FOOTBALL
What do Keith Byars, Bo Jackson, and Eric Dickerson have in common?

ILLEGAL PROCEDURES
Which two players did Commissioner Peter Rozelle suspend for the entirety of 1963 for gambling on league games?

WORLD OF THEIR OWN
Who scored the first regular season touchdown in the WLAF?

Emphasizing the unusual and the significant— never the commonly known—this tough quiz book will keep both the trivia whiz and football fanatic on the defensive. But this is your chance to take the challenge and score yourself in a full-of-fun competition that's guaranteed to make every football fan stand up and cheer!

PLUS: PAYDIRT (The answers!)

THE ALL-NEW ULTIMATE FOOTBALL QUIZ BOOK

Warren Etheredge

A SIGNET BOOK

SIGNET
Published by the Penguin Group
Penguin Books USA Inc., 375 Hudson Street,
New York, New York 10014, U.S.A.
Penguin Books Ltd, 27 Wrights Lane,
London W8 5TZ, England
Penguin Books Australia Ltd, Ringwood,
Victoria, Australia
Penguin Books Canada Ltd, 10 Alcorn Avenue,
Toronto, Ontario, Canada M4V 3B2
Penguin Books (N.Z.) Ltd, 182–190 Wairau Road,
Auckland 10, New Zealand

Penguin Books Ltd, Registered Offices:
Harmondsworth, Middlesex, England

First published by Signet, an imprint of Dutton Signet,
a division of Penguin Books USA Inc.

First Printing, August, 1993
10

Copyright © Warren Etheredge, 1993
All rights reserved

 REGISTERED TRADEMARK—MARCA REGISTRADA

Printed in the United States of America

Of fathers, I've forgotten one
and been fortunate to find another.
Thank you, Gerry.

ACKNOWLEDGMENTS

To the good people of REM Studio: my gratitude.
To Jennifer: my head, my heart, my hope,
and . . . oh, my thanks.

CONTENTS

THE COIN TOSS

Few people truly appreciate football. Fewer still, understand my love for the game. "You like football, Warren? You *watch* football?" Apparently, they are deceived by my appearance. I have no beer belly, nor bulging biceps. But I do love the game. To the layperson, it may appear to be a slap-dash, free-for-all wrestlefest, with the snap of the ball and the blow of the whistle merely marking endless bouts of legalized mayhem. But for those who have played and/or studied the game, it is obvious that football is an incredibly complex sport that demands an almost ascetic devotion to fully comprehend.

This book is for those who have realized the beauty of the game and have immersed themselves in every facet of it. The quizzes and puzzles are designed to challenge even diehard fans. The answers include additional information so that those who claim to know it all, may someday be right.

You have won the coin toss and elected to receive. Good luck!

THE ONE AND ONLY'S

For more than 20 years, football announcers repeatedly reminded their viewers during Dallas games that, "Tom Landry is the only coach the Cowboys have ever had." The one and only.

In 1989, all of that changed. Maverick businessman Jerry Jones purchased America's franchise and brought in his ol' Razorback buddy Jimmy Johnson to replace the legend and lead the squad. The transition was unceremonious and Landry's distinction was lost. Landry will always be remembered, but he is no longer the one and only.

Below, 25 questions pertaining to players, coaches, and teams that can brag about their unique status.

1. Which is the one and only team to go undefeated through both the regular and post-seasons?

2. Who is the only head coach of Hispanic descent in the National Football League?

3. Only one player has been selected as the Most Valuable Player of the Super Bowl on three separate occasions. Who has successfully "mined" three MVP trophies and four Super Bowl rings?

4. Only once in the 56-year history of the NFL draft, has a wide receiver not been selected in the first round. In which year were the wide-outs "overthrown"?

5. Which is the one and only team never to have defeated either the Oakland or Los Angeles Raiders?

6. In only one Super Bowl has a player from the losing team been selected as the game's MVP. Who was it?

7. Who is the only graduate of the University of Puget Sound to play in the NFL?

8. Which is the only team ever to field both the league's leaders in rushing and receiving yardage in the same season?

9. The Washington Redskins, despite their many gloried seasons and countless glory boys, have retired only one jersey number in the history of their franchise. What is the number and who wore it?

10. In 1991, running back Barry Sanders played in every regular-season game but one. With only

one Lion missing from their lair, how did Detroit fare?

11. Only one player has scored more than 2,000 points in his career? Who is he?

12. Only one head coach has directed his team to Super Bowl victories with three different starting quarterbacks. Who is the sideline commander and who were his winning field generals?

13. Who is the only Kansas City Chief to ever lead the league in rushing?

14. Which was the only team to not advance to the playoffs during the 1980s?

15. Only one head coach has led three different teams to divisional titles. Name the coach and his winning trifecta.

16. In only one Super Bowl have *two* players been cited for the game's MVP honors. Name the recipients and number the Super Bowl.

17. Which was the only team not involved in a single trade during the 1987 campaign?

18. Only once has a Heisman Trophy winner been drafted by that year's Lombardi Trophy winners. Identify the collegiate all-star and the Super Bowl champions who drafted him.

19. Who is the only person to have been named Coach of the Year in the World Football League, the National Football League, the United States Football League, and the NCAA's Southwest Conference? (Hint: The leagues have been ordered in accordance with this coach's résumé.)

20. Since moving from Cleveland in 1946, the Rams have won one, and only one, NFL championship. Which team did Los Angeles defeat for the title and in what year did they do so?

21. Clem Daniels retired as the AFL's career-rushing leader, despite an inauspicious beginning with the Dallas Texans. In 1960, his rookie season, Daniels carried the ball once, only once. How many yards did he gain?

22. Only once has an NFL game that has gone into overtime been decided by a safety. Which two teams were involved and who scored the decisive 2-pointer?

23. Who is the only professional football player to have died in action during the Vietnam Conflict?

24. On the day of and the days prior to the 1992 NFL Draft, only one trade was completed that included future considerations. Which two teams and which player were involved in the deal?

25. In his rookie season in the NFL, Jimmy Johnson coached Dallas to only one victory during their excruciating 1989 campaign. Which was the only team to succumb to the Cowboys and what was the game's final score?

NICKNAMES

There have been Bullets (Bob Hayes, Bill Dudley) and Sugar Bears (Ray Hamilton, Willie Young) and a bevy of Bubbas (Baker, Smith, McDowell, etc.). All were tagged affectionately, but without much flair. For simply by its utterance, the *artful* nickname evokes the image and energy of a specific individual. Say "Crazy Legs" and Elroy Hirsch's awkward stride is immediately recalled. The mere mention of "The Hammer" summons Fred Williamson and his nail-biting tackles to mind. These nicknames are as unique as the players who inspired their colorful epithets. Joe Namath will always be "Broadway"-bound, Ed Jones, forever "Too Tall," and Joe Greene, "Mean."

Listed below, 25 players, each followed by a multiple of monikers. Match each with his appropriate alias.

1. CRAIG HEYWARD
   a. The Mallet   b. Musclehead
   c. Ironhead   d. Warhead

2. JEFF HOSTETLER
   a. Adam   b. Hoss
   c. Little Joe   d. Cartwright

3. "NEON" DEION SANDERS
   a. Prime Time   b. Grandstand
   c. Box Office   d. White Shoes

4. MICHAEL IRVIN
   a. The Rainmaker b. Playboy
   c. Flash   d. The Playmaker

5. GARY CLARK, ART MONK, AND RICKY
   SANDERS
   a. The Hoglets   b. The Good Hands
                        People
   c. The Three Amigos d. The Posse

6. WILLIE ANDERSON
   a. Flipper   b. Shamu
   c. Sherwood   d. Robin Hood

7. CHRISTIAN OKOYE
   a. The Ethiopian   b. The Nigerian
      Eclipse   Nightmare
   c. The Cheboygan   d. The Nuclear Namibian
      Commando

8. REGGIE WHITE
   a. The Pass-rushing b. The Sensei of Pain
      Preacher
   c. The Minister of   d. Rabbi Red-dog
      Defense

9. DESMOND HOWARD
   a. Magic   b. Flash
   c. The Rocket   d. The Sprocket

10. RAGHIB ISMAIL
    a. The Turk   b. Call Me
    c. The Canuck   d. The Rocket

11. JAMES GEATHERS
    a. Go-To   b. Jumpy
    c. Fair Weather d. Rush

12. MARK JACKSON, VANCE JOHNSON,
    AND RICKY NATTIEL
    a. The Posse   b. The Fun Bunch
    c. The Three Amigos d. The Fly Boys

13. RED GRANGE
    a. The Galloping   b. Casper
       Ghost
    c. The Gipper   d. Dust Bowl

14. JOHN RIGGINS
    a. Hoglet   b. Jerry-rigged
    c. Pigboy   d. The Diesel

15. FRED BILETNIKOFF
    a. Blinky   b. Grumpy
    c. Specs   d. Carrots

16. HENRY WILLIAMS
    a. Stripe   b. Gizmo
    c. Gremlin   d. Beetle

17. TOM TRACY
    a. Tom Thumb   b. Tom Cat
    c. Tom the Bomb   d. Tom Terrific

18. JIM HUNT
    a. Volcano   b. Earthquake
    c. Buffalo   d. Disaster

19. CHARLES PHILYAW
    a. Godzilla   b. Jaws
    c. King Kong   d. Frankenstein

20. TOM SULLIVAN
    a. Silky   b. Smooth
    c. Moves   d. Shakes

21. CLARENCE MANDERS
    a. Pit Bull   b. Pug
    c. Boxer   d. Mutt

22. DICK BASS
    a. The String   b. The Striped
    c. The Spark Plug d. The Scooter

23. ANDY NELSON
    a. Bones   b. Scottie
    c. Doc   d. Stretcher

24. FRED EVANS
    a. Astaire   b. Rogers
    c. Dippy   d. Dancer

25. BART BUETOW
    a. The Nutty
       Professor
    c. Teach

    b. The Absentminded
       Professor
    d. The Mad Scientist

MUDDLE IN THE HUDDLE #1 (SAFETIES)

This is the first of three quizzes in which the names of 10 prominent or promising players have been encoded. Each letter below corresponds to another, for example, *w* might represent *e* and *j* might represent *b*, and so on.

As coach, it is your job to reassign the x's and o's so that the true identities of these players may be revealed. The years and teams for which each has played are included to assist you.

As there are no ladies present, safeties first!

1. YDMXM BDVBDMK
   Denver Broncos (1989–)

2. HMEEQM HRBFMY
   Detroit Lions (1988–)

3. CBKZ NBKKQMK
   Chicago Bears (1990–)

4. FMKTE NSMKKP
   Kansas City Chiefs (1981–)

5. FBXQF AORNSMK
   Cincinnati Bengals (1986–)

6. HKMDD CBLQM
   New Orleans Saints (1985–)

7. DQC CnFTEBRF
   St. Louis Cardinals (1987), Phoenix Cardinals
   (1988–)

8. MKQZ CnCQRRBE
   New York Jets (1988–)

9. RTOQY TRQXMK
   Miami Dolphins (1989–)

10. BEFKM VBDMKY
    Philadelphia Eagles (1984–)

FIRST AND TEN

This is the first of four chapters in which clues are provided to identify 25 players, past or present, memorable or forgettable. The clues become progressively more obscure as the chapters become progressively more difficult ("First and Ten"—the easiest, "Fourth and Long"—the toughest.) Identify all the players correctly, Coach, and your team will pick up the first down. Good luck!

1. This former Bear back broke many records, perhaps the "sweetest" being that for career rushing yardage.

2. After quarterbacks Joe Montana and Steve Young were felled by injuries in 1991, this no-name third-stringer stepped up to lead the 49ers to a 10–6 season.

3. The Indianapolis Colts have had little to brag about during the past few seasons, except for the perseverance and promise shown by their "franchise" quarterback.

4. This Buffalo Bill was the league leader in combined yardage from the line of scrimmage for the second straight season in 1991.

5. This Cleveland Brown defensive tackle is the brother of Chicago's "Fridge."

6. This defensive tackle was the first player chosen in the 1991 NFL draft. The University of Miami graduate was the recipient of the 1990 Outland Trophy.

7. This Packer wide receiver is never "dull." In 1989, he led the league with 90 receptions (for 1,423 yards).

8. This running back has not achieved the success the Jets had hoped for when they selected him with the second pick overall in the 1990 draft. Some speculate that his slow start and propensity for injury are a result of an improper recovery from a college ailment.

9. Prior to the 1992 season, New Orleans matched an offer sheet extended by Detroit to retain the services of their free-agent linebacker. The contract that kept this Saint sacker in the bag also made him the highest-paid defensive player in the NFL.

10. A Detroit Lion from 1980–1991, he was one of the league's most accurate kickers.

11. This wide receiver has played for the Seattle Seahawks since 1988, the same year his younger brother, a safety, signed with the Detroit Lions.

12. In 1992, the Cincinnati Bengals drafted this quarterback from Houston as the heir apparent to lefty Boomer Esiason.

13. This Houston Oiler wide-out led the league with 100 receptions in 1991.

14. Many would suggest that the Buccaneers blundered, rather than plundered, when they selected this player with the first pick overall in the 1987 draft.

15. This New York Giant was the oldest active running back playing in the NFL during the 1992 season.

16. The New England Patriots selected this running back in the first round of the 1991 NFL draft. The Arizona State graduate ranked fourth in the AFC in rushing yardage in his rookie season.

17. New England's other first-round selection of 1991 was also an impact player. This USC graduate, chosen with the eleventh pick overall, assumed a starting tackle position immediately with the Patriots.

18. In 1991, this kicker outscored the entire Indianapolis Colts' squad.

19. This Pittsburgh Steeler cornerback/kick returner was once a world-class hurdler.

20. This Buffalo Bill defensive end brags that Lawrence Taylor is no longer the premier defensive player in the NFL, because he is.

21. The Falcons used the first pick overall in the 1988 draft to select this linebacker from Auburn University. Unfortunately for Atlanta, he never developed into the Gritz-blitzer they had expected. After efforts to convert him into a defensive end, a defensive tackle, and even a tight end had failed, Jerry Glanville gave up and left him unprotected as a Plan B free agent following the 1991 season. Subsequently, he was signed by the Raiders.

22. Despite leading the league in completion percentage in 1991, this Seattle quarterback was designated a Plan B free agent by the Seahawks in the off-season. Thereafter, he signed with the Kansas City Chiefs.

23. This San Diego Charger was the first defensive lineman selected in the 1989 NFL draft. That year, he was the eighth player chosen overall.

24. This former Minnesota Viking safety has three brothers—Jim, Keith, and Ross—who have also played professionally.

25. Despite challenges from Bo Jackson and Roger Craig and Eric Dickerson, he remains the most consistent star in the Los Angeles Raiders' backfield.

SCRIMMAGED LINES #1 (DEFENSIVE LINEMEN)

A teammate nicknamed defensive tackle Randy White the "Manster." The alias was a reference to the former Cowboy's presumed hybrid nature: half man, half monster. White accepted the moniker. After all, defensive linemen frequently are called far worse. There is a common misconception among the public and even their pigskin peers, that members of the front four—perhaps due to their abnormal size and strength—are at least, part beast. With a few exceptions, this is rarely the case.

Below are the names of 27 of the NFL's most gentle "mansters." Kindly return each to his proper position in the blank crossword diagram on the facing page.

3-LETTER NAMES
Jeff ALM

Blenda GAY
Art MAY
Mel TOM

4-LETTER NAMES
Dave BUTZ
Mike GANN
Bill MAAS
Ken SIMS

5-LETTER NAMES
Tony McGEE
Mike PITTS
Leon SEALS
Garin VERIS
Joe YOUNG

6-LETTER NAMES
Lyle ALZADO
Doug MARTIN
Tim NEWTON
Tracy ROCKER
Daniel STUBBS

7-LETTER NAMES
Fred SMERLAS
Diron TALBERT

8-LETTER NAMES
Alphonso CARREKER
Bob LURTSEMA
Russell MARYLAND
Gerald ROBINSON

9-LETTER NAMES
Trace ARMSTRONG
Gary BALDINGER

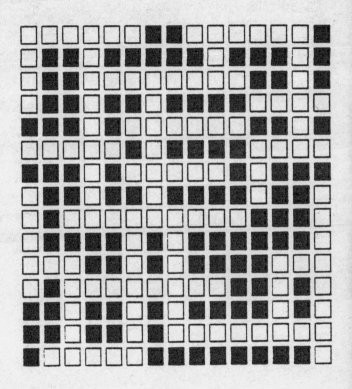

NAME FIND #1 (QUARTERBACKS)

Find the last names of the 63 quarterbacks hidden in the accompanying puzzle. (Yes, they run diagonally, too.)

Terry **BAKER**	Bobby **HEBERT**
Pete **BEATHARD**	King **HILL**
Bob **BERRY**	Don **HORN**
Steve **BONO**	John **HUARTE**
Chris **CHANDLER**	George **IZO**
Len **DAWSON**	Bert **JONES**
Benjy **DIAL**	Jeff **KEMP**
Hunter **ENIS**	Tommy **KRAMER**
Jim **EVERETT**	Dave **KRIEG**
Tom **GREENE**	Gary **LANE**
Bob **GRIESE**	Bob **LEE**
Steve **GROGAN**	Chuck **LONG**
Pat **HADEN**	Clint **LONGLEY**
John **HADL**	Dean **LOOK**
Galen **HALL**	Archie **MANNING**
James **HARRIS**	Dan **MARINO**

Dave **MAYS**
Jim **McMAHON**
Hugh **MILLEN**
Chris **MILLER**
George **MIRA**
Warren **MOON**
Earl **MORRALL**
Browning **NAGLE**
Joe **NAMATH**
Mike **NOTT**
Ken **O'BRIEN**
Mike **PAGEL**
Nick **PAPAC**
Rodney **PEETE**
Warren **RABB**
Mike **RAE**

Joe **REED**
Frank **REICH**
Timm **ROSENBACH**
Benny **RUSSELL**
Steve **SLOAN**
Butch **SONGIN**
Ken **STABLER**
Bart **STARR**
Rick **STROM**
Joe **THEISMANN**
Y. A. **TITTLE**
Johnny **UNITAS**
Billy **WADE**
Andre **WARE**
Marc **WILSON**

```
N A G L E D A W S O N I R A M
R U N E D A H A I P A P A C I
U E L T T I T R E L L I M H L
S B K R P I A E N I S A M A L
S L O A N B T L D A H O R N E
E Y G U B E L B K O O L N D N
L E A H T A M A N N I N G L E
L L L I H T A T A E O T S E E
A G L S E H Y S R G S T A R R
R N A L I A S D E E R E T B G
R O N L S R R I Z O B R I E R
O L E E M D R I M P M E K R O
M E N B A K R A M E R U H R B
R O S E N B A C H C I E R Y A
J N I G N O S O N O B R I E N
```

SCORECARD

"You can't tell the players without a scorecard!"

This enthusiastic reminder is chanted weekly by hundreds of vendors at the NFL's 14 host venues. The peanut brokers and souvenir salesmen hawk game-day programs, targeting the sport's uninitiated who need the occasional "nudge" as to which is the home team, as well as to who's wearing #12. But for those whose Sunday ritual includes either stadium-grazing or television-gazing, the program is unnecessary. The Cowboys' #12 will always be Roger the Dodger, the Jets' #12 will always be Broadway Joe, and so on.

Below, 100 players are ordered by the numbers with which their jerseys have been adorned. Following each, a few additional clues as to their identities: the position and the team(s) and the years for which they've played.

00. Center
    Oakland Raiders (1960–1974)

1. Quarterback
   Edmonton—CFL (1978–1983), Houston Oilers
   (1984–   )

2. Punter
   Philadelphia Eagles (1984–1985), Minnesota Vikings (1986), Denver Broncos (1986–)

3. Kicker
   Kansas City Chiefs (1967–1979), Green Bay Packers (1980–1983), Minnesota Vikings (1984–1985)

4. Quarterback
   Chicago Bears (1987–)

5. Punter
   New York Giants (1985–)

6. Kicker
   Chicago Bears (1985–)

7. Kicker
   New Orleans Saints (1982–)

8. Quarterback
   Dallas Cowboys (1989–)

9. Quarterback
   Detroit Lions (1989–)

10. Kicker
    Miami Dolphins (1989–)

11. Quarterback
    Los Angeles Rams (1986–)

12. Quarterback
    Atlanta Falcons (1987–)

13. Quarterback
    Miami Dolphins (1983–)

14. Quarterback
    San Diego Chargers (1973–1987)

15. Quarterback
    St. Louis Cardinals (1981–1987), Phoenix
    Cardinals (1988–1989)

16. Quarterback
    San Francisco 49ers (1979–)

17. Quarterback
    Seattle Seahawks (1980–1991), Kansas City
    Chiefs (1992–)

18. Quarterback
    Chicago Bears (1985–1990), Green Bay Packers
    (1991), Cleveland Browns (1992–)

19. Quarterback
    Cleveland Browns (1985–)

20. Running Back
    Detroit Lions (1989–)

21. Cornerback
    Atlanta Falcons (1989–)

22. Defensive Back
New York Jets (1988–)

23. Running Back
New Orleans Saints (1987–1988), Kansas City
Chiefs (1990–)

24. Running Back
Detroit Lions (1967–1973)

25. Safety
Houston Oilers (1989–)

26. Cornerback/Kick Returner
Pittsburgh Steelers (1987–)

27. Safety
Denver Broncos (1989–)

28. Cornerback
Washington Redskins (1983–)

29. Cornerback
Houston Oilers (1984–)

30. Running Back/Kick Returner
New York Giants (1989–)

31. Running Back
Green Bay Packers (1958–1966), New Orleans
Saints (1967)

32. Fullback
    Cleveland Browns (1956–1965)

33. Safety
    Cincinnati Bengals (1986–   )

34. Running Back
    Buffalo Bills (1988–   )

35. Running Back
    Chicago Bears (1986–   )

36. Safety
    Detroit Lions (1988–   )

37. Cornerback
    Buffalo Bills (1987–   )

38. Running Back
    Pittsburgh Steelers (1989–   )

39. Running Back
    Los Angeles Rams (1988–   )

40. Defensive Back
    Dallas Cowboys (1983–   )

41. Running Back
    Philadelphia Eagles (1986–   )

42. Running Back
    Cincinnati Bengals (1989–   )

43. Running Back
Washington Redskins (1969–1976)

44. Running Back
New England Patriots (1988–)

45. Cornerback
New York Giants (1987–1988), Tampa Bay
Buccaneers (1990–)

46. Tight End
New England Patriots (1989–)

47. Safety
Minnesota Vikings (1983–1991)

48. Cornerback
St. Louis Cardinals (1983–1986), Los Angeles
Raiders (1987–)

49. Safety
Denver Broncos (1981–)

50. Linebacker
Chicago Bears (1981–)

51. Linebacker
Denver Broncos (1991–)

52. Linebacker
New York Giants (1986–)

53. Center
    Indianapolis Colts (1980–)

54. Linebacker
    Detroit Lions (1988–)

55. Linebacker
    Buffalo Bills (1987–)

56. Defensive End
    Minnesota Vikings (1985–)

57. Linebacker
    Pittsburgh Steelers (1982–1988), Minnesota
    Vikings (1989–)

58. Middle Linebacker
    Pittsburgh Steelers (1974–1984)

59. Linebacker
    New York Jets (1985–)

60. Guard/Tackle
    New York Giants (1988–)

61. Guard
    Miami Dolphins (1982–)

62. Tackle
    Pittsburgh Steelers (1980–)

63. Center
    Chicaog Bears (1981–)

64. Guard
Minnesota Vikings (1988–   )

65. Guard
Detroit Lions (1988–1991)

66. Middle Linebacker
Green Bay Packers (1958–1972)

67. Guard
Denver Broncos (1989–   )

68. Offensive Lineman
Washington Redskins (1981–1991)

69. Nose Tackle
Cincinnati Bengals (1983–   )

70. Tackle
Dallas Cowboys (1967–1979)

71. Defensive End
Washington Redskins (1983–   )

72. Defensive End
St. Louis Cardinals (1987), Phoenix Cardinals
(1988–   )

73. Guard
New England Patriots (1973–1985)

74. Tackle
Chicago Bears (1983–1991)

75. Tackle
    Baltimore Colts (1983), Indianapolis Colts
    (1984–)

76. Guard
    Los Angeles Raiders (1989–)

77. Tackle
    Green Bay Packers (1989–)

78. Tackle
    Miami Dolphins (1990–)

79. Tackle
    San Francisco 49ers (1953–1963)

80. Wide Receiver
    Indianapolis Colts (1989), Atlanta Falcons
    (1990–)

81. Wide Receiver/Kick Returner
    Los Angeles Raiders (1988–)

82. Wide Receiver
    San Francisco 49ers (1987–)

83. Wide Receiver
    Los Angeles Rams (1988–)

84. Wide Receiver
    Green Bay Packers (1988–)

85. Linebacker
    Boston Patriots (1962–1968), Miami Dolphins
    (1969–1976)

86. Wide Receiver
Phoenix Cardinals (1988–   )

87. Flanker/Offensive End
Houston Oilers (1960–1966)

88. Wide Receiver
New York Jets (1985–   )

89. Special Teams/Wide Receiver
Houston Oilers (1985–1986), Buffalo Bills
(1986–   )

90. Defensive End
Kansas City Chiefs (1988–   )

91. Linebacker
Los Angeles Rams (1985–   )

92. Defensive End
Philadelphia Eagles (1985–   )

93. Nose Tackle
Detroit Lions (1987–   )

94. Linebacker/Defensive End
San Francisco 49ers (1986–1991), Dallas Cowboys (1992–   )

95. Nose Tackle
San Francisco 49ers (1984–   )

96. Defensive Tackle
    Seattle Seahawks (1990–   )

97. Defensive End
    New Orleans Saints (1990–   )

98. Defensive End
    Phoenix Cardinals (1991–   )

99. Defensive Tackle
    Philadelphia Eagles (1987–1991)

RUNNING MATES

A head coach selects his backfield pairing during the preseason; a political party elects its ticket tandem through the primary process. Throughout their respective campaigns, each will learn if they have chosen wisely. At first, the decision may not seem monumental, but should the President fall or the runner stumble, the "second-in-line" must be prepared to carry the ball, and not to fumble.

In the '70s, the mighty Miami Dolphins fielded three great runners: Larry Csonka, Jim Kiick, and Eugene "Mercury" Morris. Most teams are lucky to find just one. Listed below are the names of 20 superstar striders, past and present. Match them with their equally-abled running mates.

1. O. J. Simpson   a. Barry Wood

2. Red Grange   b. Brad Muster

3. William Andrews   c. Dan Reeves

4. Kevin Mack   d. Dalton Hilliard

5. Chuck Muncie   e. Jim Taylor

6. Franco Harris   f. Tom Rathman

7. Christian Okoye   g. Maurice Carthon

8. Ottis Anderson   h. Gerald Riggs

9. Marion Butts   i. Emerson Boozer

10. Marcus Allen   j. John L. Williams

11. Craig Heyward   k. Earnest Byner

12. Johnny Johnson   l. Bo Jackson

13. Paul Hornung   m. Bronco Nagurski

14. Neal Anderson   n. Stump Mitchell

15. Ken Willard   o. Rod Bernstine

16. Roger Craig   p. Jim Braxton

17. Rodney Hampton   q. Tony Galbreath

18. Curt Warner   r. John David Crow

19. Don Perkins   s. Anthony Thompson

20. Matt Snell   t. Rocky Bleier

MUDDLE IN THE HUDDLE #2 (TIGHT ENDS)

This is the second of three quizzes in which the names of 10 prominent or promising players have been encoded. Each letter below corresponds to another; for example, *e* might represent *v* and *a* might represent *c*, and so on.

As coach, it is your job to reassign the x's and o's so that the true identities of these players may be revealed. The years and teams for which each has played are included to assist you.

If you crack the code properly, there will be no loose ends, only tight ends.

1. QACR CILYYLI
   New Orleans Saints (1981–   )

2. CIBOL OAUWLX
   Cincinnati Bengals (1969–1976)

3. **EBUXVY KLYYLR**
Chicago Bears (1967–1969), Buffalo Bills (1970–1971)

4. **SLIILWW LKFBYKU**
Miami Dolphins (1988–   )

5. **LIVO DILLY**
Pittsburgh Steelers (1990–   )

6. **GLVXQ ZEOGUAY**
Philadelphia Eagles (1988–1991), Miami Dolphins (1992–   )

7. **CILYX ZAYLU**
San Francisco 49ers (1987–   )

8. **AHHVL YLPUAFL**
Cleveland Browns (1978–1990)

9. **ZER YAMEOLG**
St. Louis Cardinals (1985–1987), Phoenix Cardinals (1988–1989), Dallas Cowboys (1990–   )

10. **KAY PEILLY**
Washington Redskins (1979–1991)

SECOND AND EIGHT

A first down, off-tackle run by your fullback netted a mere 2-yard gain. Now, it is second down . . . 8 yards to go. Will you pass or keep it on the ground, Coach?

This is the second of four chapters in which clues are provided to identify 25 players, past or present, memorable or forgettable. Identify all the players correctly and you will pick up the first down.

1. Despite having missed what surely would have been the game-winning field goal in Super Bowl XXV, this Bill kicker was received as warmly by fans in Buffalo as he may have been by celebratory fans in New York following the game.

2. This defensive end holds the Chicago Bears' single-season record for quarterback traps.

3. This Detroit Lion's 25.8 yards per kickoff return led the league in 1991.

4. The Buccaneers did not make a selection in the first round of the 1992 draft because they had

traded their pick to the Indianapolis Colts for this quarterback. (Tampa Bay waived the infrequent starter and inconsequential backup on November 5, 1991.)

5. This Pittsburgh linebacker was named the team's Most Valuable Player for the 1991 season. The Steeler maintains his man-of-steel physique with biweekly tae kwon do classes and daily weight-room sessions.

6. This Raider running back was courageous/ stupid enough to once claim that playing behind the Colts' offensive line "is like playing Russian roulette."

7. This offensive lineman was the Oilers' first-round draft choice in 1982. In his 10 years with Houston, he has been selected for the AFC's Pro Bowl squad seven times.

8. He was once a world-record holder in the high hurdles and a wide receiver with the San Francisco 49ers.

9. In 1991, this Miami Dolphin led the league in punting when rated according to gross yardage.

10. Ranked by gross yardage, this Phoenix Cardinal finished third in the NFL's 1991 race for the punting title. Ranked by net yardage, however, he'd be #1.

11. Remarkably, the nose tackle for the Kansas City Chiefs is more difficult to block than his name is to pronounce.

12. This TCU graduate was Dallas' final pick of the 1991 draft. Despite being the team's twelfth-round selection, he wound up a starter in the Cowboys' defensive backfield by the end of his rookie season.

13. Currently, this quarterback owns the NFL record for most consecutive passing attempts without an interception.

14. This Eagle defensive back intercepted the aforementioned quarterback (question #13) to end the streak at 308.

15. As a junior, this quarterback was the 1990 Heisman Trophy winner. He played his senior year and entered the NFL draft in 1991. Regardless of the accolades, the Brigham Young graduate was not selected until the ninth round.

16. In 1991, this New England Patriot ranked a dismal 23rd in the league in punting despite having booted one 93 yards, the season's best effort.

17. His 30.6 yard average per kickoff return is the best in the history of the NFL.

18. In his 11-year career with the Washington Redskins, he started at center, guard, and tackle.

Upon his retirement, he joined Joe Gibbs' staff as an assistant to the tight ends coach.

19. This defensive lineman died on May 14, 1992, due to complications of a rare form of brain cancer. The former Bronco, Brown, and Raider blamed his demise on steroids, which he had used to enhance his physique and career.

20. Although considered by many to be the best running back available in the 1992 draft, he was not selected until the New Orleans Saints took him with the 21st pick overall.

21. This Purdue Boilermaker was Houston's first-round draft choice in 1986 (the third pick overall). Unable to sign the quarterback, the Oilers traded him on September 18, 1986, to the Los Angeles Rams.

22. In 1991, he led all NFL tight ends in receiving.

23. Today, this retired Jets quarterback is almost as famous for his knees and his commercial pitches as he once was for his stockinged legs and Super Bowl passes.

24. The Green Bay Packers have been "singing" the praises of their first-round draft choice of 1990, a linebacker from Mississippi.

25. He was the last of an era, the last to play the game of football without wearing a face mask.

THE HOLLYWOOD BOWL

In football, excellence is rewarded at every level of play, either by election to all-star squads or participation in all-star games. In high school, top players are considered All-Americans. In college, they are sent to the Blue-Gray Game or the Senior Bowl, to name just two. The pros vote their peers onto their respective AFC and NFC Pro Bowl squads.

For those players who graduate from football to filmdom, it is unlikely there will be any more honors, any more awards. It is unlikely that any will ever know Oscar or Emmy or Tony. So, to ease the transition of those running to the spotlight rather than daylight, I am inaugurating the Hollywood Bowl.

Listed below, the 11 Hollywood "stars" who comprise my all-star team. Match each "player" with his "part."

1. Lyle Alzado   a. The "cyclops giant" with an eye for Earthlings on TV's *Lost in Space.*

2. Brian Bosworth

b. A crime lord who's sent to the Lord by *The Divine Enforcer*.

3. Jim Brown

c. A cop who rules with an iron fist in *Steele's Law*.

4. Dick Butkus

d. A fishmonger and Sela Ward's ex-husband on TV's *Sisters*.

5. Rosey Grier

e. A gay informant keeping time with TV's *Hollywood Beat*.

6. Lamar Lundy

f. An ex-con named Bulk who "escorts" Vanity in *Neon City*.

7. Ed Marinaro

g. An unexpected, but politically correct, addition to *Force 10 from Navarone*.

8. John Matuszak

h. "Himself" visiting TV's favorite family, *The Brady Bunch*.

9. Ken Stabler

i. An undercover cop who infiltrates a motorcycle gang in *Stone Cold*.

10. Carl Weathers

j. A parolee who infiltrates a motorcycle gang with TV's *MacGyver*.

11. Fred Williamson

k. "Himself," a spokesperson for the "Lungbrush," on *Saturday Night Live*.

NAME FIND #2
(CENTERS)

Find the last names of the 61 centers hidden in the accompanying puzzle. (Yes, they run diagonally, too.)

Mike **ALFORD**	Blair **BUSH**
Charlie **ANE**	Mark **CANNON**
Mike **BAAB**	Jim **CLACK**
Ted **BANKER**	Rich **COADY**
Tom **BANKS**	Jim **COOPER**
Tom **BAUGH**	Eric **COYLE**
Forrest **BLUE**	Randy **CROSS**
Tom **BRAHANEY**	Dave **CROSSAN**
Pete **BROCK**	Bob **DeMARCO**

Jim **EIDSON**	Kani **KAUAHI**
Roger **ELLIS**	Alex **KROLL**
Grant **FEASEL**	Jim **LANGER**
Gerry **FEEHERY**	Chuck **LANZA**
Chris **FOOTE**	Bill **LEWIS**
Will **GRANT**	Dave **LLOYD**
Randy **GRIMES**	Ron **LOU**
Lee **GROSS**	Tommy **LYONS**
Courtney **HALL**	Don **MACEK**
Ken **HELMS**	Ken **MEDENHALL**
R. W. **HICKS**	Jon **MORRIS**
Jay **HILGENBERG**	Dan **NEAL**
Ralph **HILL**	Bart **OATES**
Fred **HOAGLIN**	Mike **ORIARD**
E. J. **HOLUB**	Jim **OTTO**
Kent **HULL**	Tom **RAFFERTY**
Ken **IMAN**	Geoff **REECE**

Bill **REID**   Chuck **THOMAS**

Dan **ROSADO**   Steve **WILSON**

Karl **RUBKE**   George **YARNO**

Bob **RUSH**   Bob **YATES**

Jesse **SAPOLU**

```
L L A H N E D E M A R C O J O
Y J E N Y E N A H A R B T A N
O D R O F L A O B O A F T H R
N M E K R O L L S U O E O O A
S A P O L U A S G D S E T A Y
K C O R B N A H A M I H N G T
N E O I Z N O S L I W E A L R
A K C A J B O E C E E R R I E
B A O R D R H U L L L Y G N F
T U Y D J Y U L A N G E R O F
H A L H H S J B C A N N O N A
O H E I I B A N K E R T S A R
M I C L E S A E F E E D S M U
A K L L O Y D A J M O R R I S
S E M I R G R E B N E G L I H
```

OUT OF BOUNDS

Officially, an NFL playing field is 120 yards long and 53⅓ yards wide. These precise borders may confine the sport; but Football, the spectacle, is a pageant that travels far outside the turf's finite realm. For across the sidelines and beyond the end zones, players roam, fans roar, and trivia rules.

Below, 20 multiple-choice questions to test your knowledge of Football . . . out of bounds!

1. As a child, Dan Fouts was a ball boy for the San Francisco 49ers?
   a. True   b. False

2. Pass-rusher extraordinaire and film buff Pat Swilling relaxes at home by watching videos on his ———— -inch home television system.
   a. 26   b. 70
   c. 96   d. 100

3. NFL players sometimes use Zylocaine during a game. Zylocaine is . . .
   a. A legal form of   b. A popular brand of
      "stickum"   chewing tobacco
   c. A sugar substitute   d. A painkiller

4. Which NFL head coach appeared on the cover of *Personal Selling Power* magazine in 1991?
   a. Sam Wyche   b. Mike Ditka
   c. Jack Pardee   d. Dennis Green

5. The Dallas Cowboys Cheerleaders have come to represent the "best" in their specialized field. For their hard work and easy good looks, each "cowgirl" received $——— for each of the 10 home games they performed at Texas Stadium during the 1991 season.
   a. $150   b. $250
   c. $15   d. $500

6. Homer Jones, formerly of the New York Giants, today is the president of Zesty Pictures, a small, New York-based film production company.
   a. True   b. False

7. Which former quarterback authored *How to Watch Pro Football on TV?*
   a. Johnny Unitas   b. Earl Morrall
   c. Rusty Hilger   d. Y. A. Tittle

8. Baseball maverick Charlie O. Finley branched out in 1991 with his reinvention of the venerable "pigskin." His version of the football has not yet been adopted by the pros, but many colleges—including Michigan—have. What does Finley's altered design feature?
   a. Day-Glo stripes   b. Hidden laces
   c. Inverted "pebbles"   d. A gyroscope

9. Joe Montana's life story has been depicted in comic book form.
   a. True   b. False

10. Which position does Katie Brown, the granddaughter of Paul Brown, currently hold in the Cincinnati Bengals' organization?
   a. Cheerleader   b. Corporate Secretary/ Legal Counsel
   c. General Manager   d. Pro Personnel Director

11. Who created the ad campaign for ESPN's 1991 schedule of Sunday night games, which featured the porcine epithet, "Pig Out!"?
   a. Steve Sabol   b. Chris Berman
   c. George Lois   d. Lex Flesher

12. Philadelphia defensive end Reggie White has authored a book entitled *The Reggie White Touch Football Playbook*.
   a. True   b. False

13. He gambled on a life after football, in . . . gambling! Which former NFL player is currently the Director of Development for Bally's in Atlantic City?
   a. Art Schlicter   b. Chalmers Tschappatt
   c. Spain Musgrove   d. Joe Pagliei

14. Which of the following billed itself as "The Official Airline of the NFL" in 1991?
   a. MGM Grand Air   b. American Airlines
   c. Northwest Airlines   d. Air Jordan

15. The body of which late, great head coach is interred at Mount Olivet Cemetery in Middletown, New Jersey?
    a. Knute Rockne   b. Paul Brown
    c. Vince Lombardi   d. Weeb Ewbank

16. Are Chicago's Mark Anthony Carrier and Tampa Bay's John Mark Carrier related?
    a. Yes   b. No

17. Which of the following four players weighed in as the heaviest during the 1991 season?
    a. Bubba Paris   b. William Perry
    c. Kevin Gogan   d. Tootie Robbins

18. The mother of which Pittsburgh Steeler was voted "Miss Turkey" of 1950?
    a. Jack Lambert   b. Bubby Brister
    c. Tunch Ilkin   d. Merril Hoge

19. Buffalo running back Thurman Thomas was absent during the Bills' opening drive of Super Bowl XXVI because he had lost his helmet.
    a. True   b. False

20. Which of the following awards did Steven Emtman *not* receive during his collegiate career at the University of Washington?
    a. The Outland   b. The Lombardi Trophy
       Trophy
    c. The Morris Trophy d. The Lombardi Award

B(U)Y THE BOOK

Aspiring all-stars, from pee-wee to professional, are raised by the book. The playbook, that is. They are expected to scrutinize and memorize the circles and squares, the curved and squiggly lines, for they will be tested on this knowledge constantly. And creativity will not count. At night, players voraciously devour pages of scribbled scrimmages and skirmishes, which they systematically regurgitate on the practice field the following day. Thus, it is no wonder that when their careers come to an end, or at least a pause, the students of the game are eager to express themselves in their own words. They are quick to evade the guidelines of the sidelines in favor of those of an autobiography's byline.

Listed below are the autobiographies of a dozen players, who could either outrun you or easily bench-press 500 pounds. So, if one of them suggests you *buy* his book, I suggest you do. For now, all I ask, is that you match these 12 titles with their respective authors (and collaborators).

1. *Audibles—My Life in Football*
   a. Roger Staubach (w/Sam Blair and Bob St. John)

2. *I Am Third*
   b. Don Strock (and Harvey Frommer)

3. *They're Playing My Game*
   c. Bill Walsh (with Glenn Dickey)

4. *The End of the Line*
   d. Hank Stram (with Lou Sahadi)

5. *First Down, Lifetime to Go*
   e. Tony Dorsett (and Harvey Frommer)

6. *Instant Replay*
   f. Leonard Marshall (with Dave Klein)

7. *One Giant Leap*
   g. Brian Bosworth (with Rick Reilly)

8. *Building a Champion*
   h. Terry Bradshaw (with Buddy Martin)

9. *Running Tough*
   i. Gale Sayers

10. *Behind the Lines*
    j. Jerry Kramer

MUDDLE IN THE HUDDLE #3 (LINEBACKERS)

This is the last of three quizzes in which the names of 10 prominent or promising players have been encoded. Each letter below corresponds to another; for example, *c* might represent *k* and *g* might represent *s,* and so on.

As coach, it is your job to reassign the x's and o's so that the true identities of these players may be revealed. The years and teams for which each has played are included to assist you.

Now, pick up the "blitz" of these anagrammatized linebackers and prove once and for all that you are a proficient code-cracker.

1. RUPAFNH PWVNZ
   Detroit Lions (1983–   )

2. CNJUY BZNNYN
   Los Angeles Rams (1985–   )

3. DUR AFZZUX
   Green Bay Packers (1986–1991), San Francisco
   49ers (1991–   )

4. XFR ATVV
   New York Giants (1956–1963), Washington
   Redskins (1964–1967, 1969)

5. JFTBAFY SWAYXWY
   New Orleans Saints (1986–   )

6. XNDA SWQYNZ
   Philadelphia Eagles (1986–   )

7. CFZH RNPCHNYLTZB
   Denver Broncos (1983–   )

8. SWAY WVVNZKFAH
   Miami Dolphins (1986–   )

9. KFZZQH DFHHNQ
   Buffalo Bills (1983–   )

10. KNZZUPC DAWRFX
    Kansas City Chiefs (1989–   )

A WORLD
OF THEIR OWN

Much like the madmen in the movies, NFL owners have long dreamed of world domination. Of course, like their silver-screen counterparts, they claim their intentions are, and their reign would be, benevolent. Their quest: simply, to indoctrinate every member of the global community as a card-carrying football fan. (Note: That's *football,* not soccer.) Though the scheme may sound insane, almost diabolical, the NFL has already launched its first and second offensives in their campaign to build a sport-homogeneous society.

Step One has birthed the American Bowl, a series of preseason exhibition contests held annually in such football towns as Tokyo, Berlin, Montreal, and Tokyo. (Mexico City may soon be a host, as well.) Step Two, the far more insidious, has unleashed the World League of American Football. The WLAF operates a 10-week spring season with 10 teams, six from the continental United States, one from Canada, and three from Europe. Although its novelty raised some interest during its rookie season, 1991, it remains a question as to whether or not the sport can be successfully exported. Their vision all-consuming, the NFL owners support their "minor" league and fight for its expansion. They live with their heads in the clouds . . . in a world of their own.

1. The World League of American Football was comprised of 10 teams in its inaugural season, 1991. In 1992, there were still 10 teams, but one of the original franchises had folded and been replaced by another. Name both squads.

2. Who was the first player chosen in the WLAF's 1992 draft?

3. This Barcelona Dragon is believed to be the first (and only?) WLAF player with his own fan club. Who is he?

4. Who holds the WLAF record for longest kick-off return?

5. Who scored the first regular-season touchdown in the WLAF?

6. Which quarterback and receiver hooked up for the longest pass play in WLAF history?

7. Former Cowboy head coach Tom Landry is a co-owner of which WLAF franchise?

8. Who holds the WLAF record for most consecutive completed passes?

9. In 1992, the NFL "loaned" 110 players to their poorer relations in the WLAF. Of those 110, how many appeared on the league's opening-day rosters?

10. Why was the start of the May 10, 1992, contest between the San Antonio Riders and the Barcelona Dragons delayed 45 minutes?

THIRD AND
THIRTEEN

Your lead-footed receiver was trapped for a 5-yard loss after you ill-advisedly called for a reverse on second down. Your team now faces a treacherous third and thirteen, Coach. What play will you call? It is an obvious passing down, isn't it? Or are you hoping that this is precisely what the defense believes, and thus, you'll opt for a delayed draw?

This is the third of four chapters in which clues are provided to identify 25 players, past or present, memorable or forgettable. Although the clues have become a little more obscure, if you can still identify all the players correctly, you will pick up the first down.

1. This tackle played a full 16-game schedule for the Cardinals in 1984, joined the USFL's Memphis Showboats for their 12-game spring season, and then rejoined the Cardinals for the entire '85 campaign.

2. The Chicago Bears and New England Patriots determined he was too small to sit in the pocket. In the CFL, however, he has stood tall. In 1991, this British Columbia Lion was honored as the league's most valuable player.

3. At 6′ 8″, he is the tallest quarterback ever to be selected in the NFL draft.

4. In 1974, he led the New England Patriots in yardage gained returning punts, returning kickoffs, rushing, and receiving.

5. This Pittsburgh Steeler cornerback played linebacker at UCLA.

6. In 1991, he became only the fourth player selected in the first round of an NFL draft by the Washington Redskins since 1968.

7. This wide receiver was a member of the U.S. 4 × 100 relay team that captured the gold medal at the 1984 Summer Olympic games in Los Angeles.

8. At these same Olympic games, this nose tackle took the silver in the shotput competition.

9. He has appeared in more Pro Bowl games than any other Philadelphia Eagle.

10. This Detroit linebacker has finished first or sec-

ond in the Lions sack totals in every season since 1986.

11. During the 1988 preseason, this Green Bay quarterback wore #5 on his uniform rather than his "magic" #7.

12. This well-traveled back is the cousin of safety Kevin Porter.

13. This Indianapolis Colt was shot and killed on May 2, 1992.

14. This running back hoped to join the U.S. Olympic karate team for the 1992 summer games.

15. This Seattle Seahawk quarterback led the WLAF's London Monarchs to the league's first championship in 1991.

16. This Alabama running back was converted to linebacker after becoming the New Orleans Saints' first first-round draft pick in 1967.

17. This 1983 Heisman Trophy winner from Nebraska played two years in the USFL before joining the Houston Oilers and, subsequently, the Atlanta Falcons, who claimed him off waivers during the 1990 season.

18. This Kansas City defensive back was the winner of the 1988 Byron "Whizzer" White Humanitarian Award.

19. This linebacker is the son of a former heavy-weight boxing champion.

20. Once a Bengals' linebacker and member of the Charter Committee of the Cincinnati City Council, he is now General Manager of the World League's New York/New Jersey Knights.

21. This running back was the New York Giants' first-round draft pick in 1971. The West Texas State graduate never fulfilled his promise and retired in 1973 after suffering a broken vertebra.

22. He beat tremendous odds in 1983 when he became the youngest player to quarterback his team to the Super Bowl. In 1992, he faced even greater odds, when illness dictated a liver transplant for this former Dolphin.

23. He was the first player to rush for 1,000 yards or more in a season for two different teams.

24. This Houston Oiler has had a tougher time off the field than on. In 1988, he sought and began treatment for a cocaine dependency problem. With that behind him, the defensive tackle spent the 1990 season recovering from a gunshot wound.

25. A fear of flying propelled this Minnesota Viking tackle to learn how to fly.

FOOTBALL
CONNECTIONS

Dick Butkus, Randy Gradishar, and Mike Croel command the respect of football's faithful. Fans will immediately acknowledge each as a terrific linebacker, but only the game's historians and the trivially obsessed will recognize the trifle that links these three, other than their terrific play.

Give up? Despite having made his name as *the* Monster of the Midway, Butkus was originally a first-round draft choice of the Denver Broncos. Only two other linebackers have been accorded this honor by the Broncos. You guessed it: Gradishar and Croel.

Below, players and teams are grouped in threes or fours. Identify the strand of insignifica that weaves each group together. (Note: The "connections" become progressively obscure.)

1. Running backs Jim Brown, Larry Csonka, Floyd Little, and Jim Nance.

2. Quarterbacks Joe Montana, Terry Bradshaw, and Bart Starr.

3. Tony Collins, Dexter Manley, and Stanley Wilson.

4. Joe Montana, Boomer Esiason, and Howie Long.

5. Deion Sanders, Brian Jordan, and D. J. Dozier.

6. Running backs Ricky Bell, Brian Piccolo, and John Cappeletti.

7. The New York Jets, the Houston Oilers, and the Denver Broncos.

8. Bill Bates, Tunch Ilkin, Hoby Brenner, and Gary Reasons.

9. Jim McMahon, Tom Landry, and Sonny Jurgenson.

10. Keith Byars, Keith Jackson, and Eric Dickerson.

GAME FILMS

A football player's lot is not an easy one. Daily, in preparation for a game, he will lift weights, work out, and scrimmage. Additionally, he will spend many hours preparing for his opponent scrutinizing films (today, videos) of his foe's previous performances. But much like the wayward student who sneaks a comic into his Chemistry textbook, I'm sure the pros occasionally sneak a peek at a full-length feature during their late-night study sessions.

Below, questions concerning 10 films that players may have slipped onto the projector, surreptitiously. Each features pro football either as a backdrop or a plot device.

Have you been doing *your* "homework"? Do you know these . . . game films?

1. In John Frankenheimer's 1977 thriller, *Black Sunday,* perennial psycho-looney Bruce Dern piloted a bomb-bearing blimp toward the Orange Bowl, an unsuspecting crowd, and an unintimidated President of the United States. Robert Shaw raced to save the day, the Prez,

and the fans from an explosive climax to which Super Bowl contest?

2. Who portrayed Elroy Hirsch in the eponymously-titled 1953 film, *Crazylegs*?

3. In which film did Billy Crystal and his buddy Bruno Kirby attend a Detroit Lions–New York Giants game at the Meadowlands? (Hint: The two unenthusiastically participated in a crowd "wave" while Crystal discussed the dissolution of his first marriage.)

4. Charlton Heston plays Ron "Cat" Catlan in Tom Gries' 1969 footbal flick, *Number One.* Catlan, an aging quarterback is besieged by marital woes and injurious blows from unbeatable foes at the helm of which NFL franchise?

5. *Paper Lion* is the true story of a writer who attended the training camp of the Detroit Lions as a "rookie" quarterback in order to gather information for an article to appear in *Sports Illustrated.* Name the author/socialite portrayed by Alan Alda in Alex March's 1968 film.

6. The road to the Super Bowl can be demanding. The length of the season and the pressure of fans and the media can be discouraging. But the competitive spirit can drive an individual to achieve the incredible. In *Heaven Can Wait,* Warren Beatty overcame the ordinary and battled the extraordinary to reach the champion-

ship game. After his "premature" cremation, the star quarterback returns from the afterlife in the bodies of first, a millionaire, and then his backup, to lead his team to the NFL title. For which professional franchise did Beatty's character compete?

7. Harry Hinkle and Willie Gingrich conspire to sue CBS, the Cleveland Browns, and Municipal Stadium after Hinkle, a television cameraman, is bowled over by a running back during a Browns–Vikings contest. Name the actors who portrayed Hinkle and Gingrich in *The Fortune Cookie.*

8. Which film features Fred Williamson as Spearchucker Jones, a former pro player called in as a "ringer" for a wartime football skirmish?

9. James Caan is a cop, tracking drug-smuggling "newcomers" in the futuristic thriller *Alien Nation,* with Mandy Patinkin. Throughout the film, he wears a T-shirt emblazoned with the name of a current NFL franchise. Of which team was Caan apparently a diehard fan?

10. In George Roy Hill's *The World According to Garp,* based on John Irving's novel of the same name, John Lithgow portrayed a former Philadelphia Eagle tight end (#90) who undergoes a sex-change operation and becomes a nurse/counselor at a hospice for abused women. What was his post-op name?

SCRIMMAGED LINES #2 (DEFENSIVE BACKS)

A defensive back always swaggers, though he sometimes staggers on the field. A wide receiver's well-run route can make the most erudite and agile DB look foolish and clumsy. Yet, even if beaten for a touchdown, the defensive back must regain his composure and take the field for the next series with the conviction that he is invincible. He may be deemed cocky, but he has to be. Lack of speed may be a liability, but, in the NFL, lack of confidence is a fatal flaw.

Below are the names of 24 of the NFL's most confident: safeties and cornerbacks. Help them "shadow" the appropriate "patterns" in the blank crossword diagram on the facing page.

3-LETTER NAMES
Carl LEE

4-LETTER NAMES
Dave AMES
Ronnie LOTT
Tommy NECK
John SISK

5-LETTER NAMES
Bill BATES
Lester HAYES
Mark KELSO
Lonnie YOUNG

6-LETTER NAMES
Bennie BLADES
Jim DUNCAN
Kenny EASLEY
Terry KINARD
Jerry LAWSON
Jesse STOKES

7-LETTER NAMES
Herb ADDERLY
Steve ATWATER
Martin BAYLESS
Mark CARRIER
Chris DISHMAN
David JOHNSON
Rod WOODSON

8-LETTER NAMES
Dick ANDERSON
Reyna THOMPSON

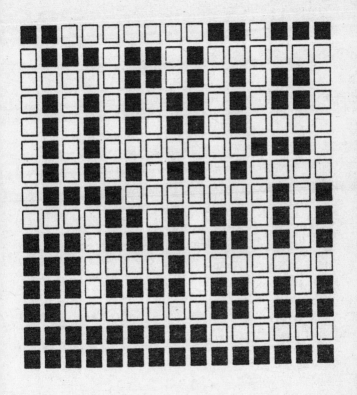

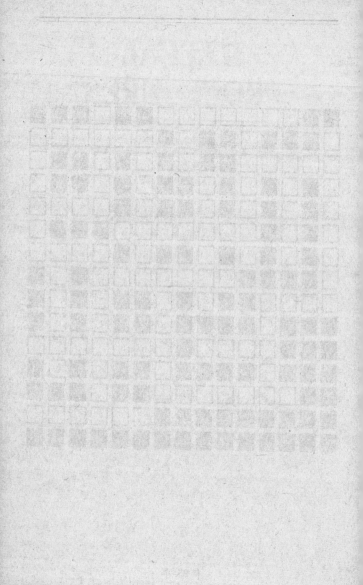

ILLEGAL PROCEDURES

In football, the most serious infractions result in the loss of 15 yards, a down, and/or ejection from the game. The consequences in real life are far more serious. Lady Justice may be blindfolded, but unlike most referees, she is not blind. And, in turn, she metes out punishment far more severely than any umpire could.

Below, 10 questions pertaining to players whose "unsportsmanlike conduct" and/or "personal fouls" have culminated and been ruled upon in . . . (il)legal procedures.

1. Litigation initiated by a single headstrong player may change the fates and fortunes of all footballers to follow. The case, heard by a Minneapolis federal district court in June 1992, may establish unrestricted free agency in the National Football League. Who filed the lawsuit?

2. Which two players did Commissioner Pete Rozelle suspend for the entirety of the 1963 season

because they had bet on the outcomes of league games?

3. In February 1992, this retired New York linebacker testified in a case brought against the Genovese crime family. Before a New Jersey State Commission of investigation, the part-owner of the Satin Dolls Lounge claimed a member of the mob "persuaded" him to pay $500 a week to "protect" his investment. Which former Giant played David in an effort to topple organized crime's Goliath?

4. Despite pleas for leniency by his former coach, Don Coryell, and teammates, this running back was sentenced to two-and-a half years in prison. Name the former Saint and Charger who was found guilty of perjury and the possession and sale of cocaine.

5. Which player sued the pay-cable station Home Box Office for "exposing" him in their postgame, locker-room coverage of the Denver Broncos–Houston Oilers 1991 AFC playoff game?

6. This defensive back received a lifetime suspension after having tested positive for a third time in a league-administered drug test. Name the Detroit Lion who was the Seattle Seahawks' first-round draft pick in 1984.

7. New Orleans' third-round draft pick in 1986, this running back missed what should have been his rookie season. In '86, the Virginia grad spent 18 weeks in jail after having been convicted on a cocaine distribution charge. Name the ex-con who began play with the Saints the following year and signed with the Chiefs as a free agent three years later.

8. True or False? The NFL fined John Elway after the Denver quarterback threw a "souvenir" ball to a wheelchair-bound fan in 1991.

9. The Dallas Cowboys' all-time leading scorer was released by America's Team a week after he had been arrested on charges of sexual misconduct with a 10-year-old girl in 1986. Name the soccer-style kicker who was as much a South-of-the-border sensation as he was a Lone Star legend.

10. During the 1987 NFL Players' Association strike, team owners fielded replacement squads to "protect the integrity of the game." The owners promised the so-called scabs all of the benefits normally accorded their unionized counterparts. Now, a class-action suit, filed in Atlanta, claims that the owners did not make good on their word. Reportedly, the owners did not allot the strike-busters severance pay upon the return of the "real" pros. Which replacement player, briefly a punter for the Atlanta Falcons, has been named the plaintiff in this lawsuit?

FOURTH AND TWO

A clutch grab by your tight end recouped 11 yards on third down, leaving you just 2 yards short of the first. A lo-o-o-ng 2 yards! Do you have the nerve to go for it, or will you trot out your unreliable kicker? Well, Coach? The fans are waiting . . .

This is the last of four chapters in which clues are provided to identify 25 players, past or present, memorable or forgettable. These clues are the most obscure, but, if you can identify all the players correctly, you will pick up the first down. (And the fans will love you, for at least one more set of downs!)

1. This graduate of the University of Florida led the Chicago Bears in rushing for six consecutive seasons.

2. He was the first Seattle Seahawk to return a kickoff for a touchdown.

3. This San Diego Charger was voted the team's Most Inspirational Player from 1988 to 1990.

4. This retired Minnesota Viking defensive lineman now is a member of Minnesota Supreme Court.

5. This offensive lineman was banned from the 1986 Citrus Bowl, which followed his senior season at USC, because he had tested positive for steroids.

6. He quarterbacked the New York Giants (1954–1959), the Dallas Cowboys (1960), and the Oakland Raiders (1962). Later, this Washington graduate served as an assistant coach with the Cowboys, Giants, Saints, Rams, Steelers, and 49ers.

7. This Buffalo Bill opened holes for "The Juice," but lost his "juice," after his agent swindled him of his football earnings. Since then, the retired lineman has worked as a high school's groundskeeper, attempted a comeback in the Arena Football League at age 40, and boxed professionally.

8. Football fanatics will remember him for his courageous contributions to the Giants as both a wide receiver and a special teams player during New York's 1986 Super Bowl season. Actress Kim Basinger cherishes another memory of him. She once remarked that the midshipman had the best butt in the NFL.

9. This offensive lineman had his number retired by the San Diego Chargers when he retired in

1969. The number was put back into circulation, however, when he returned to pro football with the Raiders in '71.

10. As a student at Woodlawn High School in Louisiana, this quarterback proved to be as proficient tossing javelins as he was tossing footballs. He set an American high school record with one such effort, which traveled 244 feet, 11 inches.

11. During halftime of the Buccaneers' December 6, 1987, encounter with the New Orleans Saints, then Tampa Bay head coach Ray Perkins punched this offensive lineman for uttering the word "quit" in his presence.

12. This defensive tackle won the 1963 Outland Trophy. The Texas Longhorn played for the Houston Oilers (1964–1966) and the San Diego Chargers (1967–1968).

13. Along with Kevin Murphy, a linebacker with the USFL's Birmingham Stallions from 1985 to 1987, this former Buffalo Bill running back founded N.E. Wear, a sportswear company, in 1991.

14. This San Diego Charger missed most of the 1990 season, having suffered severe head injuries in an assault outside a local restaurant.

15. When this Green Bay Packer rushed for 1,052 yards in 1949, he became only the third back in league history to do so.

16. This defensive lineman legally changed his name in 1977. In 1976, he played for the Jets as Larry Faulk.

17. This Philadelphia defenseman appeared on teammate Randall Cunningham's television show regularly during the 1991 season. Once, he wrestled a bull in anticipation of an impending clash with the Cowboys. Another time, he crawled around a *real* dog pound before the Eagles made their trip to Cleveland's "Dawg Pound."

18. This Redskin walked out of training camp and *announced* his retirement in 1988 in hopes of returning to his native Canada to pursue a career as a carpenter.

19. This Miami Dolphin is the grandson of Tony "The Tuna" Accardo, the reputed Chicago crime boss.

20. The Chicago Bears won the 1963 NFL Championship, defeating the New York Giants, 14–10, in the title game. The Bears' hopes for consecutive crowns were demolished, however, when they lost these two offensive stars in a tragic auto accident prior to the '64 season.

21. This tight end was the winner of the 1992 National Cutting Horse Association–NFL Super Cutting event.

22. The Buffalo brain-trust probably considered heritage as well as talent when making their eighth-round draft pick in 1990. After all, this Bill plays the same position his mother had in a professional women's league during the 1970s—linebacker.

23. He was the first NFL player to publicly declare himself a homosexual.

24. This Tampa Bay safety intercepted a pass in each of his first two regular season games and recovered a fumble in his third.

25. This Detroit dynamo was a double threat as a quarterback on the Lions' replacement team during the 1987 NFLPA strike and a pitcher in the Tiger's farm system.

NAME FIND #3
(WIDE RECEIVERS)

Find the last names of the 70 wide receivers hidden in the accompanying puzzle. (Yes, they run diagonally, too.)

Pete **ATHAS**
Stephen **BAKER**
Sanjay **BEACH**
Ken **BELL**
Tim **BERRA**
Carl **BLAND**
J. V. **CAIN**
Roger **CARR**
Mark **CARRIER**
Don **CLUNE**
Linzy **COLE**
Aaron **COX**
Paco **CRAIG**
Jerry **DAANEN**
Carroll **DALE**
Wendell **DAVIS**

Bill **DRAKE**
Mark **DUPER**
Hart Lee **DYKES**
Quinn **EARLY**
Henry **ELLARD**
Phillip **EPPS**
Bernard **FORD**
John **GARRETT**
Everett **GAY**
Jack **GEHRKE**
Frank **GRANT**
Mel **GRAY**
Roy **GREEN**
Bob **HAYES**
Freddie **HYATT**
Michael **IRVIN**

Tommy **KANE**
Jeff **KEMP**
Curtis **LEAK**
Gary **LEE**
Jerry **LEVIAS**
Leo **LEWIS**
Louis **LIPPS**
Pete **MANDLEY**
Willie **McGEE**
Ron **MORRIS**
Bobby **MOTEN**
Jimmy **ORR**
Stephone **PAIGE**
Danny **PEBBLES**
Johnny **PERKINS**
Frank **PITTS**
Bucky **POPE**
David **RAY**
Andre **REED**

Jerry **RICE**
Preston **RILEY**
Ricky **SANDERS**
Rod **SHERMAN**
Mike **SIANI**
J. T. **SMITH**
Jack **SNOW**
Paul **STAROBA**
Dwight **STONE**
Otto **STOWE**
Lynn **SWANN**
Steve **SWEENEY**
Al **SYKES**
Jim **THAXTON**
Odessa **TURNER**
Howard **TWILLEY**
Wesley **WALKER**
Bob **WEST**
Eric **YARBER**

```
S R E D N A S E L B E E P P S
E K G R A N T W I L L E Y A H
K A E A I V T O A A E L G A E
Y E H K B D I T D N A B Y C R
D L R E P O P S T O N E T O M
V E K M C G R A Y A S A H T A
P V E P O P O A H K Y C A I N
E I Q G A R R E T T E H X R D
R A N I I B R W I S U S T E L
E S I A E A A I M E I R O N E
I P V R E L P K S W E E N E Y
R E R C K F X T E P O P I E L
R A I E A C O L E R P N L R R
A R R K N N C R I N A I S G A
C L U N E N A A D D R A L L E
```

THE RED ZONE

Bend-don't-break defenses allow opponents to roam freely from 20 to 20. But once an offense crosses that line and enters "the red zone," the defense stiffens. Gaps are plugged. Runners who had seen daylight, see open holes, eclipsed by inside linebackers, turn black. Zones are flooded. Receivers who had found seams, find themselves hemmed in by nickel coverage. The offense sputters. The drive ends. The defense rests.

You have reached the red zone. Until now, the questions have been relatively easy. This chapter is the true test of your football knowledge. Answer the following 50 questions correctly and you will be trivia's reigning champion.

1. Who recorded the longest punt in the NFL in 1989? (Hint: He runs, he passes, but he doesn't normally punt.)

2. In which year was the proposal to hold an annual draft of collegiate players *accepted* by the NFL?

3. Who was the first player selected in the first NFL draft?

4. Who was the first player to be signed by the team that drafted him?

5. In which year did the NFL allow underclassmen to declare themselves eligible for the league's annual collegiate draft?

6. Which three players, as of February 1, 1992, rank as the career leaders in quarterback traps? (Note: The NFL did not begin compiling statistical information concerning sacks until 1982.)

7. Super Bowl fever must be contagious. Rapt by the attention surrounding their second consecutive appearance, Buffalo misguidedly allowed running back Thurman Thomas to skip one of the many mandatory media sessions prior to Super Bowl XXVI. The NFL fined the team for this transgression. How big was the Bills' bill?

8. Name the five men who have been inducted in the Dallas Cowboys' Ring of Honor in Texas Stadium.

9. Prior to the 1992 draft, 27 of today's 28 NFL franchises had, at one point or another, used a first-round pick to select a quarterback. Which

team made it unanimous in '92, and which quarterback did they choose?

1991 proved to be a fairy-tale season for the Lions—a Grimm's fairy tale. For although Detroit did appear blessed in reaching the NFC Championship game with the Washington Redskins, they also were cursed. During the team's playoff drive, both Mike Utley and Jerry Ball were lost to devastating injuries.

10. On November 17, 1991, Mike Utley fell freakishly during a routine pass-play blocking assignment. As a result, he will be paralyzed—permanently—from the chest down. That same day, in a contest between Houston and Cleveland, another player had to be carried off the field on a stretcher. Fortunately, he was paralyzed for only 90 minutes and not a lifetime. Name the Browns' wide-out who will walk, but never onto a football field, again.

11. Three weeks later, Jerry Ball was lost for the season during the Lions' December 8 encounter with the Jets. The All-Pro nose tackle was a victim of a chop-block which, prior to his injury, was deemed legal on running plays, though not on passing plays. Name the two New York players who, some speculate, conspired to "deflate the Ball."

12. By virtue of their 1–15 record in '91, and a clever trade with the Buccaneers, the Indianap-

olis Colts earned the first two picks of the 1992 NFL draft. Which team, in which year, was the last to corral the top two pro prospects?

13. According to NFL regulations, what is the distance between the two goal posts?

14. To whom did New York Head Coach Bill Parcells award a game ball following the Giants 39–20 thrashing of the Denver Broncos in Super Bowl XXI?

15. After polling the managerial staffs of many NFL franchises, *The Sporting News* selects its Executive of the Year. Who was awarded this honor in 1991?

16. Which NFL franchise has gone the longest without winning a league championship?

17. From 1934 through 1991, 236 players have rushed for 1,000 yards or more in a single season. Of these dashers and slashers, who holds the record for the best yards-per-carry average?

18. Which is the oldest stadium currently in use in the NFL?

19. In his four Super Bowl appearances, the 49ers' Joe Montana threw 11 touchdown passes. How many times was he intercepted?

20. On December 16, 1991, New York Jets receiver Dale Dawkins drove home after a 3–6 loss, earlier that day, to the New England Patriots. Dawkins lost control of his Nissan 300ZX after the car careened across an ice patch and rammed into a tree. Fortunately, a teammate who was following 100 yards behind witnessed the crash and rescued Dawkins from the wreck. Who is the Good Samaritan who saved Dawkins' life and, possibly, salvaged his career?

21. Former Pittsburgh Head Coach Chuck Noll has vehemently and repeatedly denied knowledge of and/or responsibility for the accusations made in *False Glory*. The book's author alleges that Noll silently condoned his and his teammates' usage of steroids during the 1980s. Name the retired Steeler lineman who put these charges in print.

22. When did the American Football League conduct its first draft of college players?

23. Which NFL legend, interviewed during the first evening of riots in Los Angeles following the announcement of the verdict in the Rodney King case, lamented: "The modern black athlete is probably the most embarrassing human being from the standpoint of reinvestment in black people that we've ever had."

24. How much did a minute of advertising time cost during Super XXVI?

25. On December 12, 1965, two teams vied for the title in the final AFL Championship game. Which teams were involved and what was the outcome?

26. A touchdown is worth 6 points; the point after adds another. A successful field goal scores 3 points and a safety increases the tally by 2. Is it then possible for an NFL team to record a victory with a 1–0 decision?

27. Each year, a parade is organized in Pasadena to celebrate the dubious achievement of the player who is the last to be selected in the NFL draft. Who was the 336th pick overall in the 1992 draft, and thus, so honored?

28. The American Football League was formed in 1959 and began play in 1960. A year later, this Chicago Bear became the first player to intentionally allow his contract to expire so that he might sign with an AFL squad. Name the offensive end who snubbed his NFL allegiance and the team for which he switched leagues.

29. In 1977, the NFL adopted its restricted free agency policy, which allows an unsigned player to receive "offer sheets" from other clubs. Should the player opt to sign an offer sheet,

his original team may retain his rights by rewarding him with an equal or better contract. If the original team forgoes this right of first refusal, the player may then switch teams, but his former squad must be compensated with draft picks. In return for "losing" a player who has more than three years of league experience and earns more than $290,000, the previous team receives two first-round draft choices. This is a steep price to pay, even for a superstar. Thus, in the 15 years the system has been in place, only five players have received offer sheets. Of those five, only two actually changed teams in exchange for draft choices. Name these two far-from-free agents.

30. The promising career of Los Angeles Raider cornerback Stacey Toran ended in a tragic auto accident. Toran was drunk when the accident occurred. California state law recognizes a blood alcohol level of .10 percent as the limit at which one will be considered to be driving under the influence. What was Toran's blood alcohol level at the time of the crash?

Although Commissioner Paul Tagliabue has delayed the expansion process, the NFL should still be adding two teams, one to each conference in the next few years. This growth will be the first for the league since Seattle and Tampa Bay were awarded franchises in 1974 (and began play in '76). Five cities remain in the hunt for an NFL berth. The following four questions pertain to those candidates.

31. James Busch Orthwein curried favor with the NFL when he bailed out Victor Kiam, the debt-plagued owner of the New England Patriots. Orthwein purchased the Patriots in 1992 and agreed to "stabilize" the organization until another suitable owner could be located. In doing so, Orthwein greatly enhanced the possibility of which former NFL city being awarded a franchise?

32. Among Orthwien's co-investors is a former NFL star who would become the league's first minority representative. Who is he?

33. Which best-selling author heads one of three parties bidding to return pro football to Baltimore?

34. Which city can take the "sting" out of NFL owners' small-town doubts by boasting that it has recently launched and supported a franchise in the National Basketball Association?

35. Who conceived the NFL's "tradition" of Thanksgiving Day games?

36. In 1992, the Raiders' maverick owner Al Davis, finally and deservedly, was elected to Pro Football's Hall of Fame. This year, he was inducted

into another Hall of Fame as well. Which was it?

37. What was the Bert Bell Benefit Bowl?

38. In 1988, 49er tackle Charlie Krueger sued the San Francisco organization and won a $2.3 million settlement. What was the nature of the charges Krueger brought against his former team?

39. Since 1960, the Raiders have played their regular season home games in six different stadiums. Name them.

40. In what year did the NFL adopt the policy that allowed teams unlimited free substitution of players?

41. Football can be a dangerous and painful sport. Bobby Hebert can testify to that. The Saints' quarterback, who suffered cartilage damage to his knee in '87 and a shoulder separation in '91, has admitted that he consulted with a physician outside the New Orleans organization to procure proper medication for these ailments. Which painkiller did his doctor prescribe?

42. In 1989, the Lions and Steelers selected running backs Barry Sanders and Tim Worley, respectively, in the first round of the NFL draft. On October 1 of that year, the two

teams clashed in an inter-conference match that pitted their freshmen in a battle for rushing supremacy. Which runner outgained the other by only a yard and what were his totals for the day?

43. During the 1920s, Rock Island fielded a professional football franchise. What was the name of that team?

44. Much ado was made of Al Davis' promotion of Art Shell to the Raiders' head coaching position in 1989. Many believe that the former all-star lineman is the first black head coach. They are wrong. Shell is merely the first black head coach of pro football's modern era. Who truly owns the distinction?

45. In their inaugural season, the AFL's New York Titans won seven games and lost seven under head coach Sammy Baugh. Despite their competitiveness, the year was marred by a loss in their encounter with the Houston Oilers on October 9, 1960. Explain.

46. What is defensive end "Natu" Tuatagaloa's full name?

47. Six Degrees of Separation, Part II? In 1992, a con man, posing as a football star, befriended singer Diane Schuur and record exec. Carl Griffin and appeared on *The Maury Povich Show*. The talk-show's topic: athletes and their

obsessive fans. Only after taping the episode did Povich and his staff realize they had been hoodwinked by one such groupie. Name the player who's caught bombs and the imposter who bombed after being caught.

48. Who is the NFL's Director of Player Programs?

49. Jim Thorpe was in demand as much in death as he was in life. After he died on March 28, 1953, two towns united to bid for and win the rights to bury the former Olympian and football legend. Citizens and politicians believed his interment would increase their revenues by attracting tourists to their previously unremarkable locale. They enshrined Thorpe in a $15,000 mausoleum of pink marble and voted to rename their towns in honor of the Native American and ex-Oorang Indian. Name the two towns and the state where Thorpe now resides.

With only seconds remaining in the game and trailing by 5 points, your team faces a fourth and goal from 1 yard out. You have no choice, Coach. You must go for it. Can you punch it into the end zone, or will a heroic goal-line stand deny you the World Championship?

50. With the imminent addition of two more franchises within the next few years, the NFL is considering the possibility of realigning teams in both conferences on the basis of geography

or rivalry or both. If so, it will not be the first time the league has juggled its formation. In 1967, the NFL concocted an unusual three-year arrangement, in which it would be divided into two conferences of two divisions each. In 1968, two teams were instructed to flip-flop their divisional placements, only to revert to their original groupings the following year. Detail the structure of the NFL in 1968, naming the conferences, the divisions, and the teams that played in each.

PAYDIRT!
(ANSWERS)

THE ONE AND ONLY'S

1. The **Miami Dolphins'** 1972 record of 17–0 remains the "perfect season."

2. In 1992, Seattle "promoted" their general manager, **Tom Flores,** to coach the Seahawks squad. Flores was formerly the head coach of the Raiders.

3. Trips to Disneyland were in order for the 49ers' **Joe Montana** who was named MVP for his performances in Super Bowls XVI, XIX, and XXIV. He had to settle for just the NFL title after Super Bowl XXIII, for which teammate Jerry Rice won the honor.

4. **1990**

5. The **Tampa Bay Buccaneers** own a 0–2–0 mark against the Silver & Black.

6. **Chuck Howley** was named the MVP of Super Bowl V. The Cowboy linebacker intercepted two passes and led a defense that held the Colts to a meager 69 yards in 31 rushing attempts. Despite his efforts, Baltimore defeated Dallas, 16–13. (Howley was also the first non-quarterback to receive the MVP trophy.)

7. Running back **Mike Oliphant** has performed with the Washington Redskins and the Cleveland Browns.

8. In 1991, **Dallas Cowboy** running back Emmit Smith led the NFL with 1,563 yards rushing. Concurrently, wide receiver Michael Irvin's 1,523 receiving yards set the league standard.

9. **#33 Sammy Baugh** anchored the Redskins' offensive and defensive backfields from 1937 to 1952. In 1960 and '61, he was the head coach of the New York Titans and in 1964, he coached the Houston Oilers.

10. Detroit advanced to the NFC Championship game in 1991, a feat no one believed possible after their regular-season opener. Without Sanders, the pride of their pride, the Lions were easily housebroken by the Washington Redskins, **45–0.**

11. Over the course of his career, **George Blanda** tallied 2,002, a football odyssey.

12. Washington's commander-in-chief, **Joe Gibbs,** prepares incredible, connect-the-dot game plans for his quarterbacks, which make them appear almost interchangeable at times. The Redskins have captured the Lombardi Trophy with **Joe Theismann** (Super Bowl XVII), **Doug Williams** (Super Bowl XXII), and **Mark Rypien** (Super Bowl XXVI), respectively, at the helm.

13. In 1989, Kansas City's **Christian Okoye** gained 1,480 yards on 370 carries. He averaged 4 yards per carry.

14. 1979 was the last year the **Balimore/Indianapolis Colts** reached the playoffs.

15. **Chuck Knox** coached the following teams to division titles (in these years): the **Los Angeles Rams** (1973–1977), the **Buffalo Bills** (1980), and the **Seattle Seahawks** (1988).

16. Defensive tackle **Randy White** and defensive end **Harvey Martin** shared the award for their contributions to the Dallas Cowboys' 27–10 victory over the Denver Broncos in **Super Bowl XII.**

17. "Let's *Not* Make a Deal" was the motto of the **Cincinnati Bengals** in 1987.

18. The **Washington Redskins** traded up to pick fourth overall in the 1992 NFL draft. They did so in order to select Michigan's **Desmond Howard.**

19. **Jack Pardee** earned his accolades with the WFL's Florida Blazers (1974), the NFL's Washington Redskins (1979), the USFL's Houston Gamblers (1984), and the NCAA's Houston Cougars (1989). He is currently employed by the NFL's Houston Oilers, who expect he will win again.

20. The Rams relocated as defending champions, but would not reclaim the NFL title for their Los Angeles fans until **1951.** Ironically, the 24–17 victory came at the expense of their successors in Cleveland, the **Browns.**

21. Clem Daniels gained no yardage. In fact, he was dropped for a **2-yard loss.** The Texans then dropped Daniels and, wisely, the Raiders recovered him. He would lead Oakland in rushing for six consecutive seasons.

22. On December 5, 1989, Viking **Mike Merriweather** blocked a punt by the Rams' Dale Hatcher. The ball rolled back through **Los Angeles'** end zone and **Minnesota** won, 23–21.

23. 6'3", 235-pound guard **Bob Kalsu** played for the Buffalo Bills in 1968 and joined the military

forces in 1969. He was killed in combat the following year.

24. Fearing the abolishment of the draft in 1993, only the **Vikings** were willing to pull the trigger on a trade. Minnesota sent defensive tackle **Keith Millard** to Seattle for the **Seahawks'** second-round pick in '92 and a conditional pick in '93.

25. On November 5, 1989, the Cowboys (and Coach Johnson) celebrated their only victory of the season, a 13–3 conquest of their division rivals, the **Washington Redskins** in R.F.K. Stadium.

NICKNAMES

1. c	8. c
2. b	9. a
3. a	10. d
4. d	11. b
5. d	12. c
6. a	13. a
7. b	14. d

15. a	21. b
16. b	22. d
17. c	23. a
18. b	24. c
19. c	25. d
20. a	

MUDDLE IN THE HUDDLE #1
(SAFETIES)

A	B	C	D	E	F	G	H	I	J	K	L	M
B	H	N	F	M	A	J	S	Q	U	Z	R	C
N	O	P	Q	R	S	T	U	V	W	X	Y	Z
E	T	W	I	K	Y	D	O	X	V	L	P	G

1. Steve Atwater

2. Bennie Blades

3. Mark Carrier

4. Deron Cherry

5. David Fulcher

6. Brett Maxie

7. Tim McDonald

8. Erik McMillan

9. Louis Oliver

10. Andre Waters

FIRST AND TEN

1. "Sweetness" himself, **Walter Payton.**

2. By now, even Bo knows **Steve Bono.** Bono's stats for 1991 (237 attempts, 141 completions, 1,617 yards, and 11 touchdowns) ranked him third in the NFC. The NFL's leading passer in '91 was teammate Steve Young.

3. If Indianapolis reaches the playoffs again someday, they will do so on the arm of Illinois graduate **Jeff George** rather than on the legs of Eric Dickerson. In 1991, the Colts' first-round pick of 1990 attempted 485 passes and completed 292 for 2,910 yards and 10 touchdowns.

4. In 1991, Buffalo's all-purpose back **Thurman Thomas** rushed 288 times for 1,407 yards and caught 62 passes for an additional 631 yards. Grand total: 2,038 yards.

5. William "The Refrigerator" Perry is only one of **Michael Dean "Gator" Perry**'s 11 siblings.

6. 6'1", 277-pound defensive tackle **Russell Maryland** didn't earn his first starting assignment with Dallas until November 17, 1991, when the Cowboys clashed with the Oilers.

7. Never "dull," **Sterling Sharpe** was the first Packer to lead the NFL in receptions since Don Hutson pulled down 47 in '45.

8. Following his junior season at Penn State, **Blair Thomas** received reconstructive surgery on his right knee. Doctors and coaches have hypothesized that, subsequently, Thomas overcompensated physically. The overdevelopment of the left side of his body consequently limited his playing time and productivity.

9. Saint linebacker **Pat Swilling** is "blessed" with talent.

10. In both 1988 and 1989, Detroit's **Eddie Murray** connected on 20 of his 21 field goal attempts, tying the NFL season record for accuracy with a 95.2 percent mark.

11. Seahawks' wide-out **Brian Blades** was born on July 24, 1965. Brother **Bennie Blades** was born on September 3, 1966.

12. Cincinnati fans hope that **David Klingler** may someday soon "restore the roar" to the Bengals' offense.

13. In 1991, Houston's **Haywood Jeffires** caught 100 passes for 1,181 yards and 7 touchdowns.

14. **Vinny Testaverde** was the last Heisman Trophy winner to be the very first pick in the NFL draft. He has never fulfilled the potential this status would suggest.

15. When St. Louis drafted him in 1979, many anticipated that **Ottis "O. J." Anderson** would be

the next O. J. Simpson. Despite several 1,000-yard seasons, no one confused him with the original O. J. and the Cardinals traded him to the Giants in '86. He may not be "The Juice," but neither has he lost "the juice." Ottis, who turned 35 on January 19, 1992, keeps on running.

16. Overall, the 14th pick of the '91 draft, **Leonard Russell** carried the ball 266 times for 959 yards, a 3.6 average, and 4 touchdowns.

17. The Pats will stand pat with Pat—**Pat Harlow,** that is. The 6' 6", 280-pound tackle should anchor New England's offensive line for years to come.

18. Redskins' kicker **Chip Lohmiller** kicked field goals and P.A.T.'s for a total of 149 points. The entire Colts' team tallied six fewer points, 143. Washington finished the season with a 14–2 record; Indianapolis went 1–15.

19. In 1984, Steeler corner **Rod Woodson** qualified for the U.S. Olympic trials in the hurdles.

20. Few would argue with **Bruce Smith**'s self-evaluation. (Except, perhaps, Reggie White.)

21. Al Davis loves projects and **Aundray Bruce**'s potential.

22. In 1991, longtime Seahawk starter **Dave Krieg** attempted 285 passes and completed 187 for a

league-high 65.6 mark, 2,080 yards and 11 touchdowns. On the downside, he threw 12 interceptions.

23. Charger defensive end **Burt Grossman** (6'6", 270 lb.) is a graduate of the University of Pittsburgh.

24. **Joey Browner** and his brothers are a little "defensive." Joey, the perennial Pro-Bowler, played safety for the Vikings 1983–1991. His brother Jim was a defensive back with the Bengals; Keith was a linebacker with the Buc's, 49ers, Raiders, and Chargers; and Ross was a defensive end with the Bengals, Gamblers, and Packers.

25. Though he may not be the flashiest, **Marcus Allen** has proven to be the most reliable Raider running back since he joined the team in 1982.

SCRIMMAGED LINES #1
(DEFENSIVE LINEMEN)

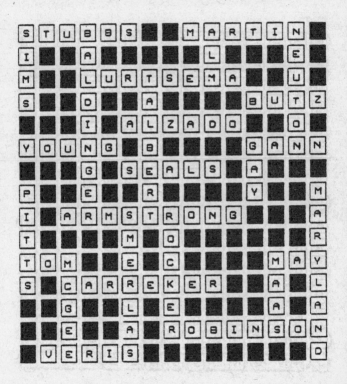

NAME FIND #1
(QUARTERBACKS)

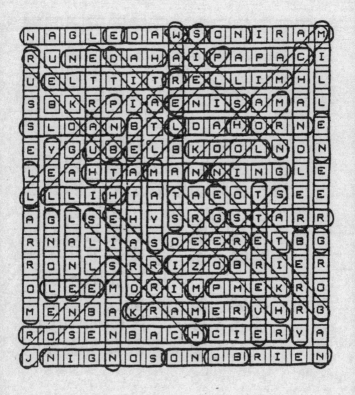

SCORECARD

00. Jim Otto

1. Warren Moon

2. Mike Horan

3. Jan Stenerud

4. Jim Harbaugh

5. Sean Landeta

6. Kevin Butler

7. Morten Andersen

8. Troy Aikman

9. Rodney Peete

10. Pete Stoyanovich

11. Jim Everett

12. Chris Miller

13. Dan Marino

14. Dan Fouts

15. Neil Lomax

16. Joe Montana

17. Dave Krieg

18. Mike Tomczak

19. Bernie Kosar

20. Barry Sanders

21. Deion Sanders

22. Erik McMillan

23. Barry Word

24. Mel Farr

25. Bubba McDowell

26. Rod Woodson

27. Steve Atwater

28. Darrell Green

29. Patrick Allen

30. Dave Meggett	46. Marv Cook
31. Jim Taylor	47. Joey Browner
32. Jim Brown	48. Lionel Washington
33. David Fulcher	49. Dennis Smith
34. Thurman Thomas	50. Mike Singletary
35. Neal Anderson	51. Mike Croel
36. Bennie Blades	52. Pepper Johnson
37. Nate Odomes	53. Ray Donaldson
38. Tim Worley	54. Chris Spielman
39. Robert Delpino	55. Cornelius Bennett
40. Bill Bates	56. Chris Doleman
41. Keith Byars	57. Mike Merriweather
42. Eric Ball	58. Jack Lambert
43. Larry Brown	59. Kyle Clifton
44. John Stephens	60. Eric Moore
45. Wayne Haddix	61. Roy Foster

62. Tunch Ilkin	79. Bob St. Clair
63. Jay Hilgenberg	80. Andre Rison
64. Randall McDaniel	81. Tim Brown
65. Eric Andolsek	82. John Taylor
66. Ray Nitschke	83. Willie Anderson
67. Doug Widell	84. Sterling Sharpe
68. Russ Grimm	85. Nick Buoniconti
69. Tim Krumrie	86. Ernie Jones
70. Rayfield Wright	87. Charley Hennigan
71. Charles Mann	88. Al Toon
72. Rod Saddler	89. Steve Tasker
73. John Hannah	90. Neil Smith
74. Jim Covert	91. Kevin Greene
75. Chris Hinton	92. Reggie White
76. Steve Wisniewski	93. Jerry Ball
77. Tony Mandarich	94. Charles Haley
78. Richmond Webb	95. Michael Carter

96. Cortez Kennedy
98. Eric Swann

97. Renaldo Turnbull
99. Jerome Brown

RUNNING MATES

1. p
2. m
3. h
4. k
5. q
6. t
7. a
8. n
9. o
10. l

11. d
12. s
13. e
14. b
15. r
16. f
17. g
18. j
19. c
20. i

MUDDLE IN THE HUDDLE #2
(TIGHT ENDS)

A	B	C	D	E	F	G	H	I	J	K	L	M
E	C	D	K	L	S	D	Q	V	Z	G	W	F
N	O	P	Q	R	S	T	U	V	W	X	Y	Z
Y	A	N	T	I	U	X	B	M	P	J	R	H

1. Hoby Brenner

3. Austin Denney

2. Bruce Coslet

4. Ferrell Edmunds

5. Eric Green

6. Keith Jackson

7. Brent Jones

8. Ozzie Newsome

9. Jay Novacek

10. Don Warren

SECOND AND EIGHT

1. Fans were particularly kind to kicker **Scott Norwood** whose last-minute attempt in Super Bowl XXV sailed wide to the right.

2. In 1984, the Bears' **Richard Dent** sacked opposing quarterbacks 17½ times. The Tennessee State grad was the MVP of Super Bowl XX.

3. Speedster **Mel Gray** returned 36 kickoffs for 929 yards in 1991. That year, he also led the league in punt returns: 25 for 385 yards and a 15.4 average.

4. Tampa Bay tried to swing a trade with the Cardinals, sending **Chris Chandler** to Phoenix in exchange for a first-round draft choice. The Cards played it cool and, reluctantly, the Buc's released Chandler whom the Cards then claimed off the waiver wire for $100.

5. 1991 MVP and Pro-Bowler **Greg Lloyd** spends two and a half hours every day pumping iron.

6. As good a runner as **Eric Dickerson** once was, it seems ill-advised for him to have made such a statement about the men who protected the ex-Colt each week from those carnivorous Lions, Bears, and Bengals.

7. Penn State's **Mike Munchak** was the eighth pick overall in the '82 draft.

8. **Renaldo "Skeets" Nehemiah** is now a member of a consortium of track and field athletes promoting the use of blood testing, in addition to urine sampling, to guarantee that the sport and its participants are not tainted by performance-enhancing drugs.

9. The Dolphins' **Reggie Roby** had a gross average of 45.7 yards. (Net average: 36.4.)

10. The Cardinals' **Rich Camarillo** averaged 45.3 yards gross per punt, and a league-leading mean of 38.9 yards net.

11. **Dan Saleaumua** was drafted by the Lions in 1987 and released following the '88 season.

(Perhaps Detroit coaches were more comfortable with the name Ball . . . Jerry Ball.)

12. Cowboy cornerback **Larry Brown** was the 320th pick overall in the 1991 draft.

13. Cleveland Brown quarterback **Bernie Kosar** threw 308 consecutive passes without once being intercepted. The old mark had been set by Bart Starr who had thrown unerringly 294 times.

14. Philadelphia's **Ben Smith** intercepted Kosar's 309th pass on November 10, 1991. Smith's pick enabled the Eagles to edge the Browns, 32–30.

15. The Green Bay Packers used the 230th pick overall in the '91 draft to select **Ty Detmer.**

16. On November 3, **Shawn McCarthy** buried the Bills in the coffin corner with his 93-yarder. In '91, the Pat punted 66 times for 2,650 yards and a 40.2 gross average.

17. **Gayle "The Kansas City Comet" Sayers.**

18. The Pro Football Hall of Fame committee elected the Redskins' versatile lineman **Russ Grimm** to the 1980's All-NFL squad.

19. Self-admittedly, **Lyle Alzado** spent an average of $30,000 a year on steroids.

20. Indiana grad **Vaughn Dunbar** will be in that number, when the Saints go marching in . . .

21. In exchange for quarterback **Jim Everett,** the Oilers received the Rams' first- and fifth-round picks in 1987 and their first-round choice in 1988. Additionally, guard Kent Hill and defensive end William Fuller were sent to Houston. In 1991, Everett ranked 27th in the league in passing with a 68.9 rating.

22. New England's **Marv Cook** caught 82 passes for 808 yards, a 9.9 average. He was the Patriots' third-round pick of the 1989 NFL draft.

23. In April 1992, **Joe Namath** had both his knees surgically replaced with artificial ones to increase his stability and decrease his pain.

24. With a name like **Tony Bennett,** the 6′1″, 234-pound linebacker may do a better job of singing his own praises.

25. **Bobby Layne** quarterbacked the Bears in 1948, the New York Bulldogs in '49, the Detroit Lions from 1950–1958, and the Pittsburgh Steelers from 1958–1962.

THE HOLLYWOOD BOWL

1. f	7. d
2. i	8. e
3. b	9. k
4. j	10. g
5. h	11. c
6. a	

NAME FIND #2
(CENTERS)

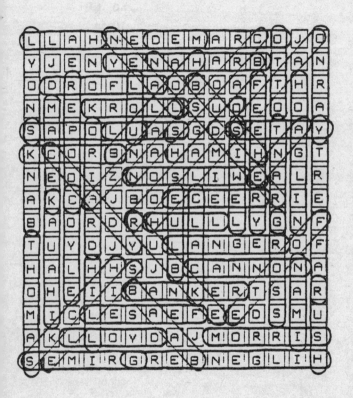

OUT OF BOUNDS

1. a. (True. Aspiring quarterbacks may apply at home-team headquarters.)

2. b. (He's not bragging. It is . . . 70 inches.)

3. d. (Zylocaine is used to deaden pain in non-weight-bearing joints.)

4. b. (Mike Ditka was the cover boy for the sales and marketing publication.)

5. c. (Only $15!)

6. b. (False. Well, they can't all be true!)

7. d. (Appearing before the title, Y. A. Tittle)

8. c. (The "pebbles" of the skin's surface are inverted so as not to protrude from the ball. Apparently, the resulting indentations enhance one's ability to catch the ball.)

9. a. (True. Montana was chosen for his animated personality.)

10. b. (Though there are plans for her someday to succeed her father, Mike Brown, as General Manager.)

11. c. (Adman George "I Want My Maypo" Lois also adopted "In Your Face" as the slogan for ESPN's '92 baseball coverage.)

12. a. (True, White is the co-author with Larry Reid. One can only assume Reggie prefers *two-hand* touch.)

13. d. (Pagliei played fullback for the Philadelphia Eagles in 1959 and the New York Titans in 1960. And yes, Tschappatt and Musgrove are real names of real players.)

14. b. (Even the Eagles, Cardinals, Seahawks, and Falcons leave the flying to American Airlines.)

15. c. (Lombardi went from Titletown, USA, to Middletown, N.J., after he died on September 3, 1970.)

16. a. (Yes. The Bear and the Buc are third cousins . . . on John Mark's mother's side of the family.)

17. b. (The winner and still champ . . . William Perry at 325 pounds! Runners-up: Tootie Robbins—322 lb., Kevin Gogan—311, and Bubba Paris—306.)

18. c. (Tunch Ilkin. Hi, Mom!)

19. a. (True, which just goes to prove today's players are unwilling to use their heads when it counts.)

20. b. (Indianapolis fans hope Steve Emtman will help the Colts capture the Lombardi Trophy, which is accorded Super Bowl champions.)

BY THE BOOK

1. k	7. l
2. i	8. c
3. d	9. e
4. f (available from Penguin USA)	10. b
	11. h
5. a	12. g
6. j	

MUDDLE IN THE HUDDLE #3 (LINEBACKERS)

A	B	C	D	E	F	G	H	I	J	K	L	M
F	L	P	K	N	V	B	A	U	S	C	H	R
N	O	P	Q	R	S	T	U	V	W	X	Y	Z
Y	W	G	I	Z	X	D	T	J	O	M	Q	E

1. Michael Cofer	6. Seth Joyner
2. Kevin Greene	7. Karl Mecklenburg
3. Tim Harris	8. John Offerdahl
4. Sam Huff	9. Darryl Talley
5. Vaughan Johnson	10. Derrick Thomas

A WORLD OF THEIR OWN

1. Spoiling the chances of **Raleigh-Durham** being selected for an NFL franchise in '94, the **Sky-hawks** played unprofessionally and were received ambivalently by Carolina fans. The team folded after a single season and was succeeded by the **Ohio Glory,** which knew no glory in '92.

2. Linebacker **George Bethune,** who played for the NFL's Los Angeles Rams in 1989 and 1990, was the first player selected in the WLAF's second annual draft.

3. Fans of Barcelona's **Eric Naposki** may show their support for the linebacker by joining "La Penya Naposki."

4. On April 26, 1992, **Cornell Burbage** of the New York/New Jersey Knights returned a kick 101 yards for a touchdown. The score helped lift

the Knights to a 34–11 victory over division foe, the Montreal Machine.

5. Nose tackle **Chris Williams** of the Frankfurt Galaxy recovered a fumble and returned it for a touchdown on the WLAF's opening weekend of play in 1991.

6. Ohio quarterback **Pat O'Hara** connected with **Melvin Patterson** for a 99-yard touchdown (and an unbeatable league record) in the Glory's 33–39 loss to the New York/New Jersey Knights on May 10, 1992.

7. Tom Landry is a member of the consortium that owns the **San Antonio Riders.** In 1992, the Riders hosted their games in San Marcos, Texas.

8. **Reggie Slack,** the quarterback of the New York/New Jersey Knights completed 16 consecutive passes. On April 12, 1992, he went 7 for 7 against the Orlando Thunder and, two weeks later, he went 9 for 9 versus the Montreal Machine. (Due to a shoulder injury, Slack did not compete in the Knights' April 18 encounter with the Frankfurt Galaxy.)

9. Only **63** of the 110 NFL "loans" were approved by the WLAF, which may indicate that the quality of play in the spring league has improved.

10. A **highway accident** involving a truck delayed Barcelona's team bus in traffic for nearly three hours. Arriving late—very late—the home team dressed and took the field without the benefit of warm-ups. The Dragons, subsequently, were extinguished 0–17.

THIRD AND THIRTEEN

1. Over the course of just 16 months, the All-Pro tackle **Luis Sharpe** competed in 44 professional league games.

2. In the States, **Doug Flutie** forever may be remembered for his heroic feats as a quarterback at Boston College. In Canada, however, his recent accomplishments have been far more dramatic and memorable. In 1991, he led the CFL in attempts, completions, and yardage. Following that season, the free agent left the Lions and signed a four-year deal with the Calgary Stampeders worth a reported $1 million a year.

3. The Seattle Seahawks drafted **Dan McGwire** in 1991 as the heir apparent to Dave Krieg. Dan is the brother of Oakland A's slugger, Mark McGwire.

4. **Mark Herron** totaled 2,444 all-purpose yards in '74, which not only led the Pats, but the league as well.

5. **Carnell Lake,** selected by the Steelers in the second round of the 1989 draft, was named the team's rookie of the year, having started in 15 of 16 games and recovered five fumbles during his first season.

6. The Washington Redskins selected 6'2", 276-pound defensive tackle **Bobby Wilson** from Michigan State with the 17th pick overall of the 1991 draft.

7. When he signed with the Raiders in 1989, wide receiver **Sam Graddy** returned to the site of his Olympic triumph, Los Angeles Memorial Coliseum, where the Raiders play their home games.

8. Since the '84 games, San Francisco's **Michael Carter** has been putting opposing centers in their place rather than putting the shot.

9. Linebacker/center **Chuck Bednarik** played for the Eagles from 1949–1962. During his 14-year career, he appeared in eight Pro Bowl games (1951–55, '57, '58, and '61) and was named the all-star contest's MVP in 1954.

10. Ferocious "lion"-backer **Michael Cofer** regularly devours opposing quarterbacks. The Tennessee graduate was Detroit's third-round selection in the 1983 draft.

11. Green Bay quarterback **Don "Magic Man" Majkowski** was paying his respect to Packer legend, Paul Hornung (who was inducted into the Pro Football Hall of Fame in 1986).

12. **James Brooks** was the Chargers first-round draft choice in 1981 and remained in San Diego until he was traded to Cincinnati in 1984. Brooks had three 1,000-yard seasons with the Bengals and joined the Browns in '92 as a Plan B free agent.

13. Defensive end **Shane Curry** was murdered in what some law-enforcement officials now speculate was a case of mistaken identity.

14. **Hershel Walker** was a member of the U.S. two-man bobsled team in the '92 Winter Games, but his plans for summer gold hit a snag when he learned America would not field a karate squad for the Barcelona games.

15. Voted the World League's Most Valuable Player in 1991, **Stan Gelbaugh** signed with Seattle prior to the '92 season to compete with Kelly Stouffer and Dan McGwire for the starter's assignment.

16. **Les Kelley** had less impact than Saint officials had hoped. The linebacker lasted only three seasons in the NFL, 1967–1969.

17. In his senior season, Cornhusker **Mike Rozier** rushed for 2,148 yards and NCAA records of 29 touchdowns and a 7.86 yards-per-carry average. He was waived by the Falcons following the '91 campaign.

18. Chiefs' safety **Deron Cherry** was honored for his "service to team, community, and country."

19. Dallas Cowboy linebacker **Ken Norton, Jr.,** is the son of . . . drumroll, please . . . Ken Norton, Sr.

20. The days and Knights of **Reggie Williams** have been very productive. The New York/New Jersey franchise, which the former linebacker fielded in 1991, advanced to the World League's championship game in its inaugural season.

21. Since his retirement, **Rocky Thompson,** born Symonds, has run a grain-exporting business in Bermuda and coached high school football in Kentucky.

22. **David Woodley** was only 24 years old in '83 when the Dolphins were scalped by the Redskins, 27–17, in Super Bowl XVII. Today, he deserves all of our prayers for a speedy recovery and a hard-earned "victory" in his battle with liver cancer.

23. In 1967, **Mike Garrett** led the Kansas City Chiefs in rushing with 1,087 yards. Five years

later (1972), he charged to 1,031 yards with San Diego.

24. By contrast, double-teams and knee injuries must seem a pleasure to **Doug Smith.**

25. 6'6", 284-pound tackle **Gary Zimmerman** played for the USFL's Los Angeles Express in 1984 and 1985, before signing with the Vikings in '86. He received his private pilot's license in 1987 and his instrument rating and own aircraft in 1990.

FOOTBALL CONNECTIONS

1. Brown, Csonka, Little, and Nance all graduated from Syracuse University.

2. Montana, Bradshaw, and Starr are the only players to have received the Super Bowl MVP award more than once.

3. Collins, Manley, and Wilson have all received lifetime suspensions from the NFL for having violated the league's drug policies in excess of three times each.

4. Montana, Esiason, and Long have all appeared as television spokespersons for Hanes sportswear.

5. Sanders, Jordan, and Dozier have all played the field—the outfield, that is—in the majors.

Sanders has roamed the field with the New York Yankees and the Atlanta Braves, his Falcon teammate Jordan with the St. Louis Cardinals, and Dozier with the New York Mets.

6. The bittersweet lives of Bell, Piccolo, and Cappeletti were each depicted in movies made for television. The films, respectively: *The Ricky Bell Story, Brian's Song,* and *Something for Joey.*

7. 1960 marked the inaugural seasons of the Jets, the Oilers, and the Broncos, as well as the New England Patriots and the Buffalo Bills.

8. Prior to the 1992 season, Bates, Ilkin, Brenner, and Reasons (along with Steve Jordan, Luis Sharpe, and Dave Duerson) were named vice-presidents on the executive board of the National Football League Players Association.

9. McMahon, Landry, and Jurgenson are all featured in Kodak's instructional videotape, "How to Play Winning Football."

10. Byars, Jackson, and Dickerson—as well as Calvin Williams and Fred Barnett—were all invited to attend a special mini-camp at the campus of Nevada-Las Vegas prior to the 1992 season, hosted and paid for by Eagles' quarterback Randall Cunningham. Cunningham invested more than $30,000 in this unorthodox preseason program, which he hoped would speed his

recovery from the knee injury he had suffered the year before.

GAME FILMS

1. Shaw thwarted the unsportsmanlike efforts of terrorists Marthe Keller and Dern, but he could not alter the outcome of **Super Bowl X**—Steelers 21, Cowboys 17. Frankenheimer intercut actual footage of the game with the film's dynamite conclusion. (Note: *Black Sunday* was based on the novel by Thomas Harris, author of *Silence of the Lambs.*)

2. Director Francis D. Lyon cast the unforgettable **Elroy "Crazylegs" Hirsch** in the title role of this very forgettable film.

3. *When Harry Met Sally.* Billy Crystal's Harry was crushed, as were the Lions, 0–20.

4. Even Charlton Heston failed to lead the **New Orleans Saints** to the promised land, the Super Bowl.

5. Alan Alda played writer/quarterback **George Plimpton,** who was much in need of a M*A*S*H unit after a few nutcracker drills with the likes of Joe Schmidt and Mike Lucci.

6. The soul of starting quarterback Joe Pendleton, in the body of backup Conrad Jarrett, took the

field and the title for the **Los Angeles Rams** with a fourth-quarter touchdown run against the Pittsburgh Steelers. Beatty portrayed both, in addition to millionaire Leo Farnsworth, in his 1978 remake of *Here Comes Mr. Jordan.*

7. **Jack Lemmon** (Hinkle) and **Walter Matthau** starred in the classic comedy directed by Billy Wilder.

8. Hawkeye Pierce and Trapper John summon "The Hammer" for a scrimmage 3 miles from the front in Robert Altman's **M*A*S*H.**

9. Though set in the future, Caan loved the team of the '70's (and '90's?), the **Dallas Cowboys.**

10. Robert Muldoon became **Roberta Muldoon,** but remained a football fan.

SCRIMMAGED LINES #2
(DEFENSIVE BACKS)

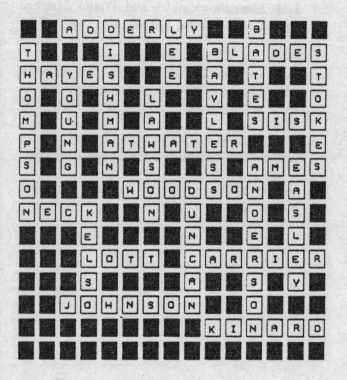

ILLEGAL PROCEDURES

1. New York Jets' running back **Freeman McNeil** claims his attempts to overturn the NFL's current system of restrictive free agency by no means expresses a personal dissatisfaction with the league or team management. He simply believes that a more equitable system for player movement must be established for the benefit of all players, not just the superstars.

2. The reputations of Detroit defensive tackle **Alex Karras** and Green Bay's "Golden Boy" **Paul Hornung** were tarnished by their yearlong suspensions. Five other members of the Lions' squad were fined $2,000 apiece for similar infractions of league policy. Neither Karras nor Hornung were found to have bet against their own teams.

3. Retired Giant linebacker **Brian Kelley** owns a one-third interest in the Lodi, New Jersey, concern.

4. **Chuck Muncie**

5. Denver wide receiver **Vance Johnson** was filmed in the buff during postgame playoff coverage in a segment on HBO's *Inside the NFL*.

6. Cornerback **Terry Taylor** was the seventh player to receive such a lifetime suspension

from the NFL. He was the 22nd player chosen overall in the '84 draft and played for the Sea-hawks through the 1988 season. In '89, Seattle traded Taylor to the Detroit Lions in exchange for running back James Jones.

7. **Barry Word** played for the Saints in 1987 and 1988 and then announced he was retiring due to his disillusionment with the pro game. He changed his mind and signed with Kansas City in 1990 and is now considered one of the NFL's finer backs. In 1991, he carried the ball 160 times for 684 yards (a 4.3 average) and 4 touchdowns.

8. **True.** Not only did the NFL fine Elway $1,000 (the league's standard fee for such an infrac-tion), the game's referee also assessed the Broncos a 5-yard penalty for the quarterback's charitable deed.

9. Mexican-bred kicker **Rafael Septien** was a hometown hero until his run-in with the law in 1986. Despite having been cleared of the most serious charges levied against him, his career in football was over. When Septien attempted a comeback with the Broncos, a group of Denver women petitioned the team not to employ him. In his nine-year tenure (1978–1986) with the Cowboys, he totaled 874 points.

10. Punter **Ralph Giacomarro,** is the named plain-tiff in the class-action suit. He, among others,

claims never to have received severance pay. (Ain't that a kick in the pants!) A U.S. District Court in Atlanta, Georgia, ruled in the players' favor.

FOURTH AND TWO

1. **Rick Casares** compiled 5,675 rushing yards with the Chicago Bears.

2. On November 13, 1983, Seattle's **Zachary Dixon** ran one back for six against the St. Louis Cardinals.

3. Charger cornerback **Gill Byrd** makes his teammates believe they can fly.

4. As a member of the Purple People Eaters' front four he laid down the law. Today, **Alan Page** practices law in Minnesota.

5. 6'4", 280-pound guard **Jeff Bregel** was the San Francisco 49ers second-round draft choice in 1987. The USC grad was the 37th player selected overall.

6. Huskie **Don Heinrich** was inducted into the College Football Hall of Fame in 1987. After his coaching stints, he went into broadcasting serving as an analyst for University of Washington, then 49er telecasts. He died on March 1, 1992.

7. Guard **Joe DeLamielleure** played with the Bills from 1973–1983 and was voted onto the AFC's Pro Bowl squad six times.

8. (Alec Baldwin, look out!) Navy grad **Phil McConkey** caught two passes for 50 yards in Super Bowl XXI, including a 6-yard touchdown reception.

9. Guard/tackle **Ron Mix** (#74) had been the only Charger other than Dan Fouts (#14) to have his number retired.

10. Although he no longer holds the record, don't feel sorry for **Terry Bradshaw;** he does own four Super Bowl rings.

11. Tackle **Ron Heller** reportedly said "let's don't quit," which rankled Coach Perkins despite the context. Perkins fractured two fingers in the off-field fracas.

12. **Scott Appleton** was the first Texas Longhorn to claim the prestigious Outland Trophy. After his retirement from football, he became a minister. He died of heart failure on March 4, 1992.

13. Kevin Murphy is the president and **Chuck Doyle,** the vice-president of N.E. Wear, a San Francisco-based clothing company that special-

izes in casual menswear. Doyle was a running back for the Bills in 1986 and 1987.

14. A jury has ruled that the restaurant outside of which **Joe Phillips** was attacked is liable for 10 percent of the damages the Charger nose tackle will receive. The jury believed that the restaurant should have provided more security in what is known to be a high-crime area.

15. Despite his fantastic '49 season, **Tony "Silver Fox" Canadeo** totaled only 4,197 yards in his 11 seasons with the Packers.

16. **Abdul Salaam** doesn't give a "faulk" what you call him.

17. Perhaps, Eagle defensive tackle **Mike Golic** will consider auditioning for the role of baseball's "Phillies Phanatic" upon retirement from the stressful world of pro football.

18. Defensive end **Marcus Koch** was ready to settle for a life down home rather than the regular home-and-away. (Apparently, he prefers planing boards to boarding planes.) But Redskin officials convinced him to return to camp, and since, has remained, and played, in Washington.

19. Regardless of his heritage, the play of defensive lineman/linebacker **Eric Kumerow** is far from criminal.

20. The Bears' title hopes were crushed when running back **Willie Galimore** (1957–1963) and end **Bo Farrington** (1960–1963) were lost in the training-camp crash.

21. It seems appropriate the event that the first-place finisher in a cutting horse competition should be a cowboy, a Dallas Cowboy, that is. **Jay Novacek** teamed with pro Bill Riddle to score 436.5 points.

22. Like mother, like son: Barbara and **Marvcus Patton.**

23. Running back **Dave Kopay** played for the San Francisco 49ers (1964–1967), the Detroit Lions (1968), the Washington Redskins (1969–1970), the New Orleans Saints (1971), and the Green Bay Packers (1972). The late, great Jerry Smith was the first player whose death has been linked to the AIDS virus.

24. **Ray Isom**

25. Forget Bo! Forget Neon Deion! What? Could it be? You've forgotten . . . **Matt Kinzer.**

NAME FIND #3
(WIDE RECEIVERS)

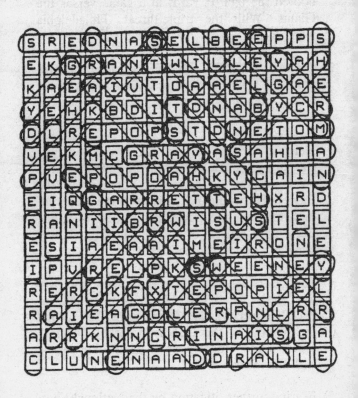

THE RED ZONE

1. **Randall Cunningham** could have cleaned up in one of those Punt, Pass, and Kick competitions! On December 3, 1989, the Eagles' quarterback booted the ball 91 yards in a game versus the Giants. With the triple-threat, Philadelphia won, 24–17.

2. On May 19, **1935,** the NFL *accepted* the proposal for teams to draft in inverse order of the teams' standings from the preceding season. The first draft was *held* on February 8, 1936.

3. Heisman Trophy-winner **Jay Berwanger** was chosen by Philadelphia, but the halfback from the University of Chicago did not sign with the Eagles. He would not sign with the Bears either, to whom the Eagles had traded his rights. Berwanger retired from football without ever playing a down, professionally.

4. After Berwanger's sudden retirement, the Boston Redskins signed blocking back/quarterback/linebacker/kicker **Riley Smith.** The second pick overall of the 1936 draft kicked 14 of 17 P.A.T.s and 4 field goals in his rookie season with the 'Skins.

5. Fearing further litigation by the National Football League Players' Association, the NFL relaxed the eligibility standards for the draft in **1990.**

6. In ascending order:

   #3. **Richard Dent**—Chicago Bears: 103½ sacks

   #2. **Reggie White**—Philadelphia Eagles: 110 sacks

   #1. **Lawrence "L. T." Taylor**—New York Giants: 121½ sacks

7. The Bills were fined **$5,000.** I'm sure there's no doubting Thomas will face the press next time.

8. The magnificent seven ride again: LB **Chuck Howley** (1961–1972), MLB **Lee Roy Jordan** (1963–1976), DT **Bob "Mr. Cowboy" Lilly** (1961–1974), QB **"Dandy" Don Meredith** (1960–1968), RB **Don Perkins** (1961–1968), CB **Mel Renfro** (1964–1977), and QB **Roger "The Dodger" Staubach** (1969–1979). Jerry Jones has extended an offer to Tom Landry to be inducted into the Ring of Honor, but Landry has refused, explaining that he has been much too busy.

9. The **Denver Broncos** employed the 25th pick overall in the 1992 draft to select UCLA's **Tommy Maddox.**

10. Oilers' safety Bubba McDowell collided with Browns wide receiver **Danny Peebles,** ending that particular play and a particularly promising career. The 25-year-old Peebles announced his retirement from football shortly thereafter.

11. **Jim Sweeney** and **Brad Baxter** and Jets head coach, Bruce Coslet have denied accusations that the chop-block and its consequences were premeditated. More important, following the '91 season, the NFL reviewed and altered its chop-block policy, making such blocks below the waist illegal regardless of whether it is a passing or running play.

12. The **Chicago Cardinals** selected first and second in the **1958** draft.

13. The measure between the uprights is **24 feet.**

14. **No one** received a game ball. Coach Parcells believed that the victory was the result of a giant team effort and that everyone was equally deserving of the honor.

15. Buffalo's **Bill Polian** was the recipient . . . again. The Bills' General Manager was named TSN's Executive of the Year in 1988 also.

16. The **Cardinals,** then of Chicago, defeated the Philadelphia Eagles 28–21 for the **1947** NFL Championship. The Cardinals failed to reach a title game after moving to St. Louis, but hope to rise from the ashes during their incarnation in Phoenix.

17. In 1934, the Chicago Bears' **Beattie Feathers** became the first player to top the 1,000-yard mark, rushing 101 times for 1,004 yards. His

9.94 yards per carry that year set a standard unapproached by any superstar since. Feathers' closest challenge came from the legendary Jim Brown, who could muster only 6.4 yards per carry in '63.

18. Erected in 1924, **Los Angeles Memorial Coliseum** has been called home by both the Rams and the Raiders. The Coliseum was also the site of the 1964 and 1984 Olympic Games.

19. **None.** Joe Montana amassed 1,142 yard passing in Super Bowls XVI, XIX, XXIII, and XXIV without throwing to the other team.

20. Though his Nissan was totaled, Dawkins may still have a future in football, thanks to the heroic efforts of fellow wide-out and friend, **Rob Moore.** Dawkins escaped the crash with a shattered femur, which required the insertion of a steel rod in his right leg.

21. **Steve Courson**

22. The AFL held its first draft—of 33 rounds!—on **November 22, 1959.** It held an additional draft 10 days later on December 2 of 20 rounds.

23. **Jim Brown** made his remarks in a taped interview, which appeared on ESPN's *SportsCenter.*

24. For 60 seconds of air time, sponsors paid **$1.7 million.** In 1974, a minute cost advertisers only $217,000.

25. **The Buffalo Bills trampled the San Diego Chargers 23–0.**

26. If an NFL squad is forced to **forfeit** a contest, the game will be logged as a 1-point triumph for the unchallenged opponents.

27. Michigan center **Matt Elliot,** the 336th pick overall, may be just the man Joe Gibbs needs to keep the Redskins on top in the NFL.

28. End **Willard Dewveall** played for the NFL's Chicago Bears in 1959 and 1960. In '61, he struck "black gold" and signed with the AFL's **Houston Oilers.** He "drilled" with the team through the 1964 season.

29. Defensive back **Norm Thompson** left the Baltimore Colts to sign with the St. Louis Cardinals in 1977, the first year of the restricted free agency reform. Eleven years later, Chicago Bear linebacker **Wilber Marshall** earned the nickname "Steve Austin" when he signed a contract with the Washington Redskins, which reportedly made him a "Six Million Dollar Man."

30. Stacy Toran's blood alcohol level was a shocking **.32 percent.** (A blood alcohol level of .40

percent is considered lethal. At that percentage, the average human being fatally succumbs to alcohol poisoning.)

31. James (Anheuser) Busch Orthwein is the majority owner of a group hoping to return pro football to **St. Louis, Missouri.**

32. If Orthwein can woo the NFL to St. Loo, **Walter Payton**'s dreams will come true. Orthwein has already selected "Sweetness" to be the team's representative to the league.

33. **Tom Clancy,** the author of *The Hunt for Red October* and *A Clear and Present Danger,* hopes that the only *Patriot Games* he'll be concerned with in the near future are those between New England and his Baltimore squad.

34. **Charlotte, North Carolina,** has enthusiastically backed the NBA's fledgling franchise, the Hornets.

35. We should all give thanks to **G. A. Richards,** the first owner of the Detroit Lions, for giving us an excuse to not speak to family.

36. Al Davis is also a member of the prestigious **Adelphi University Athletic Hall of Fame** in Garden City, New York.

37. The Bert Bell Benefit Bowl, established in 1961, pitted the second-place finishers from

each conference of the National Football League in a consolation contest. Also known as **The Playoff Bowl,** the first (January 7, 1961) featured the Detroit Lions and the Cleveland Browns. The Lions triumphed 17–16.

38. Charlie Krueger, who played for the 'Niners from 1959 through 1973, claimed that he was both physically and psychologically scarred by the team's mistreatment. Apparently, the training staff did not alert Krueger as to the severity of injuries suffered and placated any concern and masked any pain by feeding him a mix of steroids and painkillers. As a result, he is now **permanently disabled.** He has also been diagnosed as having **"depressive neurosis,"** the latter condition due to a sense of betrayal.

39. These are the sites the Raiders have called home: **Kezar Stadium** (1960), **Candlestick Park** (1961), **Youell Field** (1962–1965), the **Oakland Coliseum** (1966–1981), **California Memorial Stadium** (one game in 1973), and **Los Angeles Memorial Coliseum** (1982–?).

40. The NFL began permitting unlimited substitution in **1950.** This signaled the twilight of the two-way player and the dawn of the situation-specialist.

41. **Darvocet**

42. **Barry Sanders** won the duel, carrying the ball five times for only a single yard. Yes, one yard

more than Worley, who gained zero yards on five attempts also. Despite Sanders' workhorse performance, the Lions were defeated, 3–23.

43. **The Rock Island Independents**

44. Tailback/blocking back **Fritz Pollard** was a player-coach for the Akron Pros (three stints: 1920–1921, 1925, 1926), the Milwaukee Badgers (1922), and the Hammond Pros (1923–1925).

45. The Oilers defeated the Titans that day, 27–21. But far more devastating for the Titans was the loss they suffered as a consequence of the contest. New York guard **Howard Glenn died as a result of a broken neck** incurred during the game.

46. Natu's birth name is more than a mouthful: **Gerardus Mauritius Natuitasina Tuatagaloa.**

47. It's a bird, it's a plane, it's New York Giants' wide receiver **Mark Ingram**—NOT! Con man **Aaron Williams** was exposed after members of the Povich staff contacted Giant officials for background information and learned that the real Mark Ingram had been in Detroit the day of the show's taping. Whoops! The show never aired in its original form.

48. On May 11, 1992, NFL Commissioner Paul Tagliabue appointed **Dr. Len Burnham** as the league's Director of Player Programs.

49. Jim Thorpe has done his part; his body remains in the Jim Thorpe Monument in Jim Thorpe, **Pennsylvania.** Regardless of his presence, few consider what were once the townships of **Mauch Chunk and East Mauch Chunk** in their summer travel plans.

50. It is important to remember that in 1968 the NFL had yet to merge with the AFL, and thus:

THE NATIONAL FOOTBALL LEAGUE

EASTERN CONFERENCE

CAPITOL DIVISION
Dallas Cowboys
New York Giants*
Philadelphia Eagles
Washington Redskins

CENTURY DIVISION
Cleveland Browns
New Orleans Saints*
Pittsburgh Steelers
St. Louis Cardinals

WESTERN CONFERENCE

CENTRAL DIVISION
Chicago Bears
Detroit Lions
Green Bay Packers
Minnesota Vikings

COASTAL DIVISION
Atlanta Falcons
Baltimore Colts
Los Angeles Rams
San Francisco 49ers

*The Giants and the Saints were the teams that swapped divisions in '69

LAST MAN OUT
by Donald Honig

It is February, 1946, in New York. The sensational base-ball rookie Harvey Tippen has just signed on with the Dodgers. Everything is going great until fate throws a sharp curve. A gorgeous, young society heiress is found brutally murdered, and Tippen, who was her last lover, is now tops on the suspect list. Agonizing over a secret he is afraid to confess, Tippen is caught between cops look-ing for a quick conviction and a Dodger ownership seek-ing to sweep the scandal under the carpet. It looks like Tippen's diamond future is over before it's begun when baseball reporter Joe Tinker sends the game into extra innings. But nothing can prepare Tinker for what awaits him at the end of this twisted trail of desire as he hunts for the truth and tries to persuade the police that a vital piece in the puzzle has been overlooked. Ringing with authenticity, this mystery-thriller is as rich in nostalgic magic as it is in spellbinding suspense.

Coming from Dutton Books

27 million Americans can't read a bedtime story to a child.

It's because 27 million adults in this country simply can't read.

Functional illiteracy has reached one out of five Americans. It robs them of even the simplest of human pleasures, like reading a fairy tale to a child.

You can change all this by joining the fight against illiteracy.

Call the Coalition for Literacy at toll-free **1-800-228-8813** and volunteer.

Volunteer Against Illiteracy. The only degree you need is a degree of caring.